PENGUIN
COMPASS

JOURNEY TO THE WELL

Bishop Vashti Murphy McKenzie is the first female bishop of the African Methodist Episcopal Church. Her most recent pulpit was at Payne Memorial AME Church in Baltimore. She is also the national chaplain for the Delta Sigma Theta Sorority. She is the author of *Not Without a Struggle* and *Strength in the Struggle: Leadership Development for Women*. She is married to former NBA forward Stan McKenzie, and they have three children. Bishop McKenzie divides her time between Maryland and South Africa.

Journey to the Well

12 Lessons on Personal Transformation

BISHOP VASHTI M. McKENZIE

Penguin Compass

PENGUIN COMPASS

Published by the Penguin Group
Penguin Putnam Inc., 375 Hudson Street, New York, New York 10014, U.S.A.
Penguin Books Ltd, 80 Strand, London WC2R 0RL, England
Penguin Books Australia Ltd, 250 Camberwell Road, Camberwell, Victoria 3124, Australia
Penguin Books Canada Ltd, 10 Alcorn Avenue, Toronto, Ontario, Canada M4V 3B2
Penguin Books India (P) Ltd, 11 Community Centre,
Panchsheel Park, New Delhi – 110 017, India
Penguin Books (N.Z.) Ltd, Cnr Rosedale and Airborne Roads,
Albany, Auckland, New Zealand
Penguin Books (South Africa) (Pty) Ltd, 24 Sturdee Avenue,
Rosebank, Johannesburg 2196, South Africa

Penguin Books Ltd, Registered Offices:
Harmondsworth, Middlesex, England

First published in the United States of America by Viking Compass,
a member of Penguin Putnam Inc. 2002
Published in Penguin Compass 2003

1 3 5 7 10 9 8 6 4 2

Produced in association with Urban Ministries, Inc., Chicago, Illinois.

Excerpts from *The Holy Bible, New International Version*, Zondervan Publishing House.
Copyright 1973, 1978, 1984 by International Bible Society.

THE LIBRARY OF CONGRESS HAS CATALOGED
THE HARDCOVER EDITION AS FOLLOWS:

McKenzie, Vashti M., 1947–
Journey to the well / Vashti M. McKenzie.
p.   cm.
Includes bibliographical references.
ISBN 0-670-88484-7 (hc.)
ISBN 0 14 21.96207 (pbk.)
1. Christian women—Religious life.   2. Samaritan woman (biblical figure).   I. Title.
BV4527.M412   2001
248.8'43—dc21   2001056825

UMI ISBN 0-940955-77-6

Printed in the United States of America
Set in OPTI Administer Light
Designed by Jaye Zimet

To
The Circle of Love
Payne Memorial AME Church
and
Oak Street AME Church

Acknowledgments

There is not enough paper and ink to give honor to the multitude of people I am compelled to acknowledge. Many people have contributed in tangible ways to my life and this book. I am grateful to the many preachers whose sermons inspired and the mentors whose prodding motivated. I am thankful for editors whose patience bordered upon virtue. I cherish the friends whose fellowship nurtured and encouraged. I celebrate the anointed Sisters of the Covenant, who continually pray for all of us. I owe so much to my family, who is always there for me. I bow down to worship and adore a Savior whose grace allows me to exist.

I desire to express special appreciation to Payne Memorial AME Church and Dr. Jeremiah Wright and the Trinity United Church of Christ family who first heard the genesis of the *Journey to the Well*. I dedicate this book to the Circle of Love, a women's Bible fellowship, seeking Godly answers to daily challenges through study and prayer, in two of the congregations I served, Payne Memorial and Oak Street AME Churches. These two remarkable groups of women were the initial groups to have this well experience. We journeyed to the well every second and fourth Monday evenings and realized the transforming power of the Divine.

I treasure my sister-friend Kim Sadler, who first believed in this rendering of a Samaritan woman's tale; Adrienne Ingrum, who pried this story from me; to Rev. Jeff Wright, Dr. Banks and the UMI family for opportunity; Rev. Angelique Mason, who held down the fort; Gayle Aldrich for her rescuing abilities; to Carolyn Carlson and the Penguin Putnam Group for giving this Samaritan woman a place to be heard.

I thank God daily for my husband, Stan, who allows me to spread eagle wings and fly as far as the Divine allows. I appreciate the fruit of my womb whose presence is a joy in our life. I give honor to those to whom honor and credit are due.

Vashti Murphy McKenzie

Contents

Journey to the Well

Preface

$\backsim$

My mother read a story to me every night when I was growing up. I wonder now if her philosophy was "a story a day keeps ignorance away." I cherish that old, worn book of children's tales; the cover has faded, and the binding has loosened its grip on many of the pages. I am puzzled that a vibrant, beautiful single woman named Snow White fell for seven quirky dwarfs. Another story had me believing that one day a handsome prince would find my comatose body in my urban wilderness and awaken me with a happily-ever-after kiss. I even put a pea under my mattress to see if I was a princess in disguise. But I never had enough hair to tempt a lover to climb my tresses to the second floor of my Baltimore city row house. As a lanky Olive Oyl teenager whose feet, front teeth, and ears were too big for her body, I believed with all my heart the ugly duckling story. Under my pimples I knew a swan was waiting to be released. As a high school senior, I read books such as *Hiroshima*, which taught me that every story has two sides. *Man's Search for Meaning*, which I first encountered as a college freshman, showed that we weren't the only people to be touched by oppression. Lorraine Hansberry's *A Raisin in the Sun* displayed hope struggling to survive in hostile territory. The movie *Philadelphia* later provoked compassion for those facing HIV and AIDS.

For generations my family members told one particularly powerful story around our dinner table. The story was about how our family's weekly newspaper got started when my great-grandfather, John H. Murphy, Sr., borrowed two hundred dollars of his wife's butter-and-egg money to purchase the printing equipment of a failed enterprise. He had published the *Sunday School Helper* for years in the basement of Bethel AME Church in Baltimore, and in 1887 began the *Afro-American Newspaper* when only .5 percent of African Americans could read. The newspaper grew to become one of the largest chains of black weekly newspapers in the country, and more than one hundred years later family members still own and manage the Afro-American Newspaper Company. What this story taught me was that if a whitewasher could become a newspaper-publishing giant, then anyone could become whatever he or she chose to become.

I love a good story. Stories have power to teach, train, inspire, motivate, encourage, and change minds, habits, and perceptions. Stories have the power to teach lessons when previous efforts have failed. Stories create nonthreatening environments that promote receptivity. They allow a listener or reader to take sides: Would you act as the protagonist does or would you second-guess the villain, hero, or heroine? While it's often all too easy to ignore the advice of parents, priests, spouses, counselors, and friends, a good story can get under one's skin to influence and change behavior. Biblical stories, like the story of the Samaritan woman meeting Jesus at the well, are more than fairy tales and fantasy; they are Divine stories that have the power to touch the heart, mind, and soul. These Divine stories transcend culture and time to speak to many generations all over the world. It is through an awakening, or the conversion experience, that we are able to transcend habit, history, and heritage. These biblical power-lifts are makeovers more powerful than any new hairstyle; they are transforming experiences that lead us to our God-given Created Purpose. These stories are lessons in living life on purpose.

The story of the Samaritan woman reveals that personal transformation takes place when individuals are willing to spend time with God, investing self, time, energy, and personal reflection, in the process of calling up and meditating on past events to move beyond limiting barriers. The woman at the well is a good story, but not an ordinary story. Hidden beneath a simple account of self-discovery and Divine revelation is a powerful story of personal transformation. This is the tale of one woman's encounter with Jesus the Christ at Jacob's well one afternoon. Her transition from a woman with a suspicious lifestyle to a woman proclaiming the Good News is a dramatic one. What a story! This is a story that can lead to our own personal transformation. By studying and learning more about the story of the many Samaritan women, our lives can also be transformed through listening to Christ's words. Many Samaritan women? you may be asking. Yes, there is only one physical woman at the well, but she has many women inside her, as we will discover.

Inside each of us is at least one unseen woman. She sings when she wants to, writes poetry, dreams of Broadway plays she will one day perform if only she can find the nerve to be an actor's actor like Alfre Woodard. She writes great novels, dances with Alvin Ailey, plays the piano at Carnegie Hall, paints in watercolors all day, and works in charcoal at night. On a good day, she is hopeful when her sisters are fearful. She has purpose when others are confused, is unusual when routine is no longer comfortable, is creative when faced with the ordinary, and revolutionary when evolution is too slow.

As women, we are sometimes defined by one role: mother, daughter, teacher, executive, wife, sister, architect, or pharmacist, rather than as a collage of many women kneaded into one like yeast kneaded into fresh dough. We see ourselves as one image, one composition, one photograph, one Kodak moment at a time. We present ourselves to the world as one woman at a time, letting all the other women inside us starve for attention. We are one woman with many different aspects, just as the Body of Christ is one body with many parts. As there is one God in three persons, we are one with many facets. The women inside us make up our individual unique collage. We are pieces of this, a fragment of that, a segment here, and a section there. Sometimes we forget that we are mother, sister, aunt, grandmother, wife, friend, and daughter at the same time that we are worker, supervisor, politician, paralegal, homemaker, financial expert, agent, advocate, personal banker, poet, teacher, artist, storyteller, disciple, minister of reconciliation, and ambassador of Christ. Many women live inside us, starved for attention. These women slip through now and then like a petticoat peeking below the edges of a hemline. They come forward when all issues are settled: homework, housework, yard work, commuting, computing, faxing, e-mailing, shopping, kissing, kidding, and tucking away the young and old.

These other women inside of us are hidden by the demands of work, standing in the constant shadow of our responsible selves, taking a backseat to the woman who must work to eat, give to live, pay bills, and hold up her end of a relationship. Like shadows in a darkened room, they become visible only when the light is turned on, when they shine with every shift of the light source. There is not enough time in the day for them to roam freely, and they come forward only when their conscious, responsible, accountable selves have seen to everyone else's needs. They emerge when the house is still and quiet around them. They go to bed early, but remain awake listening to the thoughts of their unconscious breaking through to the conscious mind. One woman is sorting laundry while another wanders the halls of her own intellect looking for places to apply lessons learned. Another languishes in a state of self-neglect and indifference to others, while yet another cries waterless tears because her fragility has too often been caught in the vise of relationships. Many women live inside us, the many facets of our being, forced into hiding by a world challenged by diversity. These women inside of us are waiting to be set free. They are the brokenhearted waiting to be mended, the grief stricken waiting for the oil of joy to replace their tears.

Examine the collage of Maya Angelou: poet, author, playwright, composer, film director, friend, singer, mother, and organizer. Look at the collage of Oprah Winfrey: talk-show host, television producer, film producer, singer, songwriter, actor, innovator, friend, lover, entrepreneur, angel, and broadcast journalist. Consider the collage of Leonardo da Vinci: anatomist, architect, scientist, musician, costume designer, stage designer, botanist, painter, city planner, philosopher, inventor, geographer, mathematician, engineer, humorist, chef, physicist, and raconteur. Inspect the collage of Marion Wright Edleman. She is author, children's advocate, wife, mother, organizer, detail tender, activist, keynote speaker, and fund-raiser. Contemplate the collage of Condoleeza Rice: daughter, pianist, presidential adviser, and foreign policy analyst. Each woman within our personal collage is a chapter in the story of our lives, and each of these women contributes to the others. One woman doesn't threaten another, since each one is necessary to our story and one woman connects us to the next woman. Each represents a significant stage, moment, or development in life, but we will not get the entire picture until we step back and view the collage as a whole. One piece of the collage does not tell the whole story; each piece in the collage is a chapter in the story.

Well women are women who challenge a Kodak moment. You are more than a photograph or a portrait; you are a collage, an art form where many different objects and materials are assembled on a canvas or board. These various pieces are placed together to create a multidimensional thought, theme, image, or impression, and often when the whole collage is complete it contains materials that wouldn't ordinarily be used in the same composition. A collage can look like the artist is confused, as if she started out working in one medium and ended up working in another; the material used is only limited by the artist's imagination. People who like things organized, matched, or balanced may have difficulty working in the mixed-media world of collage. It takes many different pieces to tell a whole story. Yet when carefully arranged these pieces tell a unique story. The women inside you make up your collage, your collection of experiences juxtaposed with one another. It doesn't always look like these women fit together and some of the pieces are as different as night and day, but when you pull them together it begins to make sense. The collage represents the sum of the whole, and it is hard to tell the whole story without all its parts.

Celebrate your many selves instead of locking them away in a closet like Christmas ornaments in summer or last summer's sandals in winter. Well women in the making, you can look for and choose carefully the pieces you want to add to your own collage—not just accept the pieces life gives you. In the end, a collage representing the many women on the inside of you will emerge.

The journey to the well is a journey of faith. The Chinese use the bamboo plant as a symbol of faith: then plant it, water it, and nurture it for years even though little growth occurs. It grows excruciatingly slowly, and then suddenly, maybe in about the fifth year, it shoots up profusely. Faith waters a plant that shows little progress; faith keeps pouring water on the roots until change takes place. You will need faith, daughters of the well, to keep focused on your journey until you begin to grow profusely and celebrate *all* the women inside you. On the outside, it won't look like anything is going on, but change is taking place. The God who calls you to the well knows you better than you know yourself; the God who meets you at the well is acquainted with all the women of your virtual reality; and it is God who will give you the courage to come to the well. It is faith that will keep you coming back until you are transformed into a unique desert flower, blossoming into your Created Purpose, which you will learn more about toward the end of our journey together. Be open and receptive, because more than just water is available. Dip your cups deep into the cistern of spiritual refreshment, into the ever-flowing blessings of God. The details and particulars of our stories may differ, but the woman of Samaria is every woman who has ever hoped that someday things would change; and we all know that there is something and someone in all of our many lives that could stand a little change. Her story is our story, and our story is her story. Let us learn about what will happen on our journey to the well. We can take this journey and find ourselves transformed.

Part of transformation involves opening ourselves up to it; part of it involves developing discipline. Let me share my tips about making this a journey that will be the transforming trip for you that it has been for me.

Introduction

Journey to the Well features the Discipline of the Well, a process to assist you in getting all you can from the experience at Jacob's well. You can read this book without doing the discipline, but you will be better blessed if you do. Discipline of the Well is an invitation to discipline the mind and spirit, launching you on your own journey as you take full advantage of the Samaritan woman's experience. The Discipline of the Well can take as little as twenty minutes per day or as much as an hour. You might want to start with a small amount of time and increase it as you go along.

Begin by identifying your own space. Every woman should have a private, personal space; it does not matter whether you live alone or in a crowd. The size of your living quarters is not important—just choose a room, corner, space around a chair or table, tool shed, garden hut, greenhouse, garage, bedroom, or even the bathroom. It does not matter, as long as it is your space. Whenever you occupy your space everyone should know that they must leave you alone there; this may require up-front negotiations with spouses, children, or roommates. Helping family members identify their own personal spaces may be another way to negotiate your space and teach them to respect yours as you respect theirs. Even the youngest in the family can learn to be still and appreciate personal space. Some women may have to rise before dawn to gain privacy in their spaces, and mothers may only have access to their spaces after children are put to bed. Be encouraged, even when the amount of time is brief. Your own space is as close to being sacrosanct as you can get. It is as inviolable as the loft of the artist, the office of the chief justice of the Supreme Court, the Oval Office in the White House, or a pastor's office when she or he is in meditation or consultation. No sneaking a peak at your family's private thoughts. Tempting as it may be, you will need every ounce of patience you can muster to teach them not to read your private thoughts, letters, or books unless invited. Books left open, journals unlocked, and notes lying around are begging to be read. Help others respect your belongings and your privacy. Whatever you need to do to acquire and occupy your own space, do it. Today my space is a study where I keep books, videos, audiotapes, a computer, candles, and journals that collect my thoughts. The dog, however, still manages to resist negotiation incentives and knows how to scratch on the door to gain entrance and keep me company in the study. In past years, my personal space has been the guest bedroom, a corner of our bedroom, the family room when everyone is asleep, or the corner of the living room before everyone is awake. The nightstand on my side of the bed is also sacrosanct and holds the books I'm currently reading, magazines I'll get to one day, and newspaper clippings. The first inklings of many sermons have come to me in the middle of the night when I linger in the twilight between consciousness and unconsciousness. Notes are preserved on paper napkins, file cards, legal pads, or whatever piece of paper is handy. In a household of five people it takes negotiation to secure permanent personal space, but I can love my family better if they give me twenty minutes for personal spiritual discipline. It may be difficult at first, but it is not impossible.

The Discipline of the Well is learning to say no to some things, so that we're able to say yes to important things by turning away from certain aspects of life and turning toward the spiritual disciplines. It is the process of smoothing out rough edges, correcting ragged activities, and adjusting your appetites. The root system of the California redwood is shallow and gains strength by clumping together, linking roots that spread out across the surface. The palm tree has a different root system. Its roots go deeper than those of most trees in order to anchor it securely when the winds blow hardest. The deep roots serve to draw nourishment from sources far below the surface and the palm tree is able to survive in the bleakest desert climate because of its root system. The Discipline of the Well will help you construct deeply rooted, Christlike qualities. These character roots will help you overcome the old and new challenges around you. Shallow roots have their virtues, but deep roots anchored by spiritual discipline stand the test of time.

Discipline is the simple ordering and organizing of behavior according to a specific structure with a determined outcome in mind. It is usually undermined by our love-hate relationship with it. We love disciplined children and yet we hate to take the time to discipline them. We love the disciplined precision of a marching band, yet we hate the rehearsals needed to gain perfection. We love to see a disciplined classroom, yet we hardly spend enough time on classroom management. We love to see disciplined athletes at the top of their game, but we would hate to invest the time and energy in training ourselves. We love the discipline of soldiers in parade or a concert musician who must shut out the world and sacrifice much to practice for her or his performance. Discipline gets us up in the morning and to work on time. It takes discipline to practice, rehearse, train, diet, exercise, write, read, accomplish goals, and complete tasks. Without discipline, we would miss many opportunities. We cannot live up to our full human potential without discipline. Undisciplined minds produce chaotic lifestyles; undisciplined behavior impedes prioritizing, creating, achieving, succeeding, surviving, thriving, and envisioning. Marathon runners learn to focus on the finish line and not the crowd as they discipline themselves to run 26.2 miles on various terrains in all kinds of weather. They develop their own racing styles and are not influenced by competitors.

There are five parts to the Discipline of the Well that you may choose to practice at the end of each chapter to enhance your journey: Well Lessons, Well Words, Well Sabbatical, Well Language, and Well Work. Well Lessons and Well Words should be included as you study each chapter. The other parts of the Discipline of the Well can be done separately, or as you read through the journey. Other supplies needed include:

- *A travel log—a journal or notebook to record your own personal experiences and thoughts daily*
- *Bible—preferably New International Version (NIV)*
- *File cards—three by five or five by seven*
- *Felt-tip pens—choose colors you absolutely adore*
- *Material to build your own personal collage—poster board, paper, cork, glue, envelopes to collect objects, clippings, and photos/images of your various women*
- *Specified time—starting with five and working up to at least twenty minutes per day to work the Discipline of the Well*

Well Lessons

Each chapter will feature Well Lessons to help capture and interpret the meaning of the Samaritan woman's experience. Just as the foundation of a building serves to support the structure, Well Lessons are the foundation of the Discipline of the Well and will help you frame your own experience as you review and reflect upon the lessons from the well at the end of each chapter. The desert experience the Samaritan woman struggled through can benefit us today if we are willing to learn from her and her story. This is an opportunity to walk in her shoes, feel the sands beneath your feet, breathe the hot air, feel the intensity of the sun, taste the water, and lean upon the walls of the well with Jesus. It's not always necessary to physically experience everything when you can benefit from someone else's struggle. How would you feel? How did she feel? What would you do or what have you done differently? What can you glean from the lesson for yourself?

Well Words

Well Words serve as your landmarks; they are biblical references that will guide you during your journey. Too often the mind gets fed and the spirit is starved. God's Word will lead you and provide nourishment to your spirit when you feed upon the power of the Word. The Word of God will be ". . . a lamp to my feet and a light for my path" (Psalm 119:105, NIV). All biblical quotes are from the New International Version unless otherwise noted. I use the NIV translation because I appreciate its easily understood modern English. One of the most important elements of a journey is the map that shows the way, demarcating a path from start to finish. When you go to a different country you need a different map. The Bible is your map for the journey, and Well Words are the landmarks. Well Words are the biblical guides that will frame your experience at the well and direct you to your destiny in the desert.

Landmarks are visible, conspicuous objects that act as guides for a journey. You may not know the exact address of your destination; all you know are the landmarks. How many times have you given directions by using the landmark system? "Just go down this road until you see the fast food store. Keep going until you see a gas station on the left. Turn right until you see a row of houses. Go three houses, two trash cans, and four rosebushes, until you see the dog in the yard—that is the house you are looking for!"

Well Sabbatical

The Well Sabbatical is a time to dwell on the word of God and be still in prayerful reflection upon the Well Lesson at the end of each chapter. The

Well Sabbatical allows thoughts to surface that wouldn't otherwise stand a chance in the regular flow of your day. It allows you to slow down the pace and disconnect from the daily grind for an intentional period of rest and reflection. The responsible woman, the necessary woman, the pragmatic woman, the impatient woman, and the pity-party woman need a break. The nurturing woman, the practical woman, and the over committed woman need respite. A sabbatical is not a slumbering event or naptime (which are not altogether bad concepts). Rather, it is a wide-awake retreat from pressing deadlines, tight schedules, and full agendas, established as a period for guided quiet time when thoughts are focused upon a specific biblical text or theme, the stepping stones, or landmarks, found in each chapter.

The root from which the word "sabbatical" is derived means a regular time or season for rest. In the Ten Commandments, the seventh day was set aside as a day of rest and was observed as the Sabbath by Jews in ancient times. They rested the land and vineyards in the sabbatical year, or every seventh year; debtors were released in the sabbatical year. Today regular cycles of study and travel given to college professors are called sabbaticals. A sabbatical in the Discipline of the Well is a regular period of rest and reflection. It is more than just a pause in the day or a moment of meditation. It is a total disconnect from the daily grind for an intentional period of time with no television, radio, or music playing. Unplug the telephone, turn off the pager and the cell phone, and find a comfortable spot in your personal space. It may be on the floor, lying either on your back or stomach, or reclining in a comfortable place, feet up or head back. Just begin to see the world from a different position. You may need to put up your DO NOT DISTURB sign. My family had a habit of finding me during sabbatical time; they would see me and just begin talking, forcing me to break my silence, flooding my mind with the clutter of everyday affairs. I developed a signal: a raised index finger. When I flashed my signal, it meant I was on sabbatical and was not to be disturbed unless someone was dying or the house was burning down. A sister friend of mine ties a scarf on the doorknob of the room she uses as her sabbatical space. Another friend leaves her shoes outside the door. The overstuffed chair that usually faces the center of the room is turned to the wall when another friend is taking a sabbatical; when she can't be seen sitting in the chair, everyone in the house knows not to disturb her.

The sabbatical begins with relaxation. Take deep breaths softly and slowly until all you hear is silence. Many women may feel uncomfortable doing nothing more than listening to the silence, smelling the atmosphere, and tasting the moments as they pass by, but in the first few moments of calm composure, ideas, possibilities, and other musings that don't stand a chance at any other time of the day begin rising to the surface. It is amazing what you hear when you acquaint yourself with silence. The creative woman, the peaceful woman, the artistic woman, and the visionary woman emerge from the closet of your mind. The enterprising woman, the resourceful woman, and the tranquil woman find voices, and the innovative woman and the imaginative queen begin ruling your conscious mind. Listen to them as they reset your table with new concepts buried for years under the everyday dishes and linens of existence.

The sabbatical is a time to move out of the flow of the world and into the flow of the spiritual; you find time to do whatever you believe you want or need to do. Often more time is spent on working, eating, sleeping, and watching television than on most other daily activities. In comparison, the time spent on spiritual pursuits is minuscule. The call to rest is biblically given: "Come to me, all you who are weary and burdened, and I will give you rest" (Matthew 11:28). "There remains, then, a Sabbath-rest for the people of God" (Hebrews 4:9). "Be still, and know that I am God" (Psalm 46:10).

Initially, break your five-minute sabbatical into five one-minute segments. The first minute is to still the body and mind, breathing slowly. The second minute is to open the spirit to communication with God; the communication is called prayer and is intimate conversation with the Divine. In the Christian tradition, prayer is ended in Jesus' name. The third minute is spent listening. The fourth minute is spent reading the Well Words at the end of each chapter. The fifth minute is spent focusing your thoughts on those directives. As you grow comfortable taking sabbaticals, gradually extend your quiet time. Always end your sabbatical by recording your thoughts in your travel log or well journal.

In your journey, try morning sabbaticals. "In the morning, O Lord, you hear my voice; in the morning I lay my requests before you and wait in expectation" (Psalm 5:3). Like spring, mornings are special times of beginning; the buds of potential are on our trees of life, possibilities are blooming in the garden, and the air is fresh with goodness and mercy. Mornings are ripe with ideas ready to be harvested as the ideas rush to your conscious mind from the unconscious where they languished during your sleep. The mountain at midnight is shown to be a molehill in the dawn. The sunlight of a new day reveals that the dead of night is not a sickness leading to death. Plan on doing your sabbatical in the morning for at least seven days even if it means you must rise twenty to thirty minutes before your usual wake-up time. A morning sabbatical gives you an opportunity to be still before the business of the day. This does not mean you will not take additional sabbaticals during the day. Whenever it becomes necessary or you feel the need to slow down your harried life, you can. Reflect upon these scriptures and allow them to motivate your morning sabbaticals:

> Because of the Lord's great love we are not consumed, for his compassions never fail. They are new every morning; great is your faithfulness.
>
> LAMENTATIONS 3:22-23

> . . . weeping may remain for a night, but rejoicing comes in the morning.
>
> PSALM 30:5

> It is good to praise the Lord and make music to your name, O Most High, to proclaim your love in the morning and your faithfulness at night.
>
> PSALM 92:1-2

Well Language

Whenever you journey beyond your borders, you'll need to speak the language of the land. Well Language is the vocabulary of the journey used to support you in the exercises with positive, practical affirmations, keeping you focused on the new territory ahead, the Land of Transformation. It is important to use the right language, or you can undo all the Well Lessons, Well Sabbaticals, and Well Works you have accomplished by talking yourself out of doing what needs to be done. Your language can negate an otherwise positive experience. Well Language is your encouragement exercise, made up of positive affirmations that are reflective of the Well Lessons and Well Words, and when used daily they affirm the lessons of your journey to Jacob's well. These affirmations will help keep your spirit firm, as push-ups and pull-ups help firm the body. Firm muscles keep body parts contained within the structure set aside for them in the human body. Firm upper arm muscles are attractive in the summertime in sleeveless outfits, firm thigh muscles help the legs look great on the beach and support body weight. Strong stomach muscles help keep the girdle away, and firm back muscles help keep good posture. The positive language of the journey will help you recall lessons, bringing back concrete issues, with simple sentences that elevate the spiritual meaning of each chapter. An excellent way to affirm your experience at the well is to copy your favorite Well Language onto three-by-five or five-by-seven file cards using a felt-tip pen in an ink color you absolutely adore. Put the file cards in places you frequent daily—on your dresser, nightstand, refrigerator door, bathroom mirror, or in your lunch box. Use Well Language to encourage others and entice them to join you on the journey by sharing your affirmations with family members, coworkers, and friends. Take five minutes daily to start.

Well Work

The Discipline of the Well provides you with an opportunity to put into action and apply the Well Lessons through the footwork of the journey called Well Work. These are simple, practical exercises to help you practice what you've learned and enter deeper into the journey through your own experience. It is one thing to say you grasp the meaning of an issue, it's another thing to demonstrate what you learn in your daily life. Doing deepens the discipline, and these positive, practical applications will stretch you to perform the tasks as your transformation is demonstrated in concrete activities. Choose one or more Well Works to do during a day, during lunch and nonpeak hours of the day, or in the evening. Plan ahead to achieve maximum gain and keep studying the lessons until you complete each one at the end of the chapters. For starters, take five minutes daily. You will hit some and miss some, but it's important to keep trying until it finally hits home. Once you have learned it, pass it on by teaching it to someone else.

The prophet Daniel prayed every morning and every evening in a hostile environment. For forty days and nights Moses, the Exodus liberator, prayed and fasted on Mount Sinai. It took discipline. Gideon's army was cut down from thirty-two thousand men to three hundred because only three hundred were disciplined; the lesser but stronger number was needed more than the greater for victory in battle against their enemies. Joshua led Israel silently around the walls of Jericho for seven days and when they were ordered to wait for the command to shout, they waited; the walls fell without loss of life, but it took discipline. Jesus prayed in the Garden of Gethsemane while his three top disciples fell asleep. Discipline is what some define as obedience, home training, and more. It is what people exercise to gain control over their lives.

Color of the Journey

Scientists have concluded that color affects mood and behavior. Electromagnetic wavelengths of light radiate from the sun, making a broad spectrum of visible colors from yellow to orange, green to blue, indigo to violet. Some types of color are invisible to the eye: ultraviolet and infrared. Color guides and teaches us as it shifts wavelengths of visible light around us, on us, and within us. An apple reflects a shade of red to the retina of the eye, forming impulses that travel as coded messages to the brain. Hormones are released, altering metabolism, as well as sleeping, feeding, and temperature patterns. Every color has a personality. We don't notice colors, we feel them: Mentally, emotionally, and spiritually, color empowers us. Ancient Egyptians and Greeks used colors to heal a variety of physical and emotional disorders, using remedies from colored mineral stones, crystals, colored fabrics, ointments, and other things as healing systems. We talk in color; we feel blue with sadness, green with jealousy, and see red when angry. Color can enhance and inspire, promote healing and health, relaxation, and protection. In the Discipline of the Well we will keep a travel log, a journal to write in with colors that speak to our spirit at that moment. Use pens that reflect the color of the moment to write Well Language on file cards and collect material for your collage using envelopes and folders in colors that are meaningful. To choose the color of the moment, stand in front of a color and allow your eyes to absorb the feel of the color. How does it feel? Does it soothe or excite? Does it appeal to you? Does it say yes to you? If it does, then choose that as your color of the moment. Change your color at any time.

At the end of the regular sabbatical rest period, each traveler should take the opportunity to record her thoughts in a travel log or journal.

I

A Woman with One Hope

But if we hope for what we do not yet have, we wait for it patiently.

ROMANS 8:25

Who hopes for what he already has?

ROMANS 8:24

The gospel writer John tells the story of the woman of Samaria in John 4:4–30, 39:

> *Now he had to go through Samaria. So he came to a town in Samaria called Sychar, near the plot of ground Jacob had given to his son Joseph. Jacob's well was there, and Jesus, tired as he was from the journey, sat down by the well.*
>
> *It was about the sixth hour. When a Samaritan woman came to draw water, Jesus said to her, "Will you give me a drink?" (His disciples had gone into the town to buy food.)*
>
> *The Samaritan woman said to him, "You are a Jew and I am a Samaritan woman. How can you ask me for a drink?" (For Jews do not associate with Samaritans.)*
>
> *Jesus answered her, "If you knew the gift of God and who it is*

that asks you for a drink, you would have asked him and he would have given you living water."

"Sir," the woman said, "you have nothing to draw with and the well is deep. Where can you get this living water? Are you greater than our father Jacob, who gave us the well and drank from it himself, as did also his sons and his flocks and herds?"

Jesus answered, "Everyone who drinks this water will be thirsty again, but whoever drinks the water I give him will never thirst. Indeed, the water I give him will become in him a spring of water welling up to eternal life."

The woman said to him, "Sir, give me this water so that I won't get thirsty and have to keep coming here to draw water."

He told her, "Go, call your husband and come back."

"I have no husband," she replied.

Jesus said to her, "You are right when you say you have no husband. The fact is, you have had five husbands, and the man you now have is not your husband. What you have just said is quite true."

"Sir," the woman said, "I can see that you are a prophet. Our fathers worshiped on this mountain, but you Jews claim that the place where we must worship is in Jerusalem."

Jesus declared, "Believe me, woman, a time is coming when you will worship the Father neither on this mountain nor in Jerusalem. You Samaritans worship what you do not know; we worship what we do know, for salvation is from the Jews. Yet a time is coming and has now come when the true worshipers will worship the Father in spirit and truth, for they are the kind of worshipers the Father seeks. God is spirit, and his worshipers must worship in spirit and in truth."

The woman said, "I know that Messiah" (called Christ) "is coming. When he comes, he will explain everything to us."

Then Jesus declared, "I who speak to you am he."

Just then his disciples returned and were surprised to find him

talking with a woman. But no one asked, "What do you want?" or
"Why are you talking to her?"

Then, leaving her water jar, the woman went back to the town
and said to the people, "Come, see a man who told me everything I
ever did. Could this be the Christ?" They came out of the town and
made their way toward him.

Many of the Samaritans from that town believed in him because
of the woman's testimony, "He told me everything I ever did."

The Samaritan woman, on a mission to get water from Jacob's well, is
down to her last hope. She walks toward the well at the hottest time of
the day, avoiding people, heat penetrating the ordinary weave of her
robe, her face covered in adherence to her tradition's codes, and her eyes
lowered in accordance with her culture's norms. All alone, she steps
through swirls of dust as her hands clutch an empty clay pot carrying
one hope: the hope that one day things will change. In spite of having
five failed relationships, having no one to count on, having few remaining relationship options, male or female, and having one last hope—that
one day things will change—she keeps going. She holds on to her one last
hope. She takes the journey and continues with her regular, routine responsibilities. She goes to the well, where she encounters Jesus, and on
this most ordinary of errands, something extraordinary happens, and
her life is transformed.

The story we find in John 4 is about a woman who took a journey to
get a drink of water. She went back home without the water she had
come for, but received Living Water that changed her heart, mind, and
spirit. She left her water pots at the well, returning to town with an opportunity and purpose to preach one sermon: "Come see a man who told
me everything about myself."

Several weeks before my due date, I was a woman with one hope. I
went into full labor on the highway 150 miles from the hospital where I
had planned to have my baby. In those moments of excruciating labor,

my one hope was to get home to the hospital I was familiar with, and the medical professionals I knew and trusted with the delivery of this child. Since the baby from our previous pregnancy had died six weeks before the due date, I was praying this pregnancy through especially hard, while tackling the responsibilities of being a minister leading two churches. As I rushed toward the hospital, I was down to my last hope.

We all have a hope, we all have longed-for dreams, ideas, visions, and beliefs that keep faith alive in our hearts (Hebrews 11:1, KJV). The Samaritan woman's story is our story, and our story is the same as the stories of the rainbow women of many different hues who live all over the world. They speak different languages, adhere to different traditions, and are from many nations, clans, tribes, and environments, but all share the same hope: that one day things will change. We each carry our pots of hope to the well searching for enough water to sustain our hopes, and daily, like the Samaritan woman, we shoulder our water-toting responsibilities, making the necessary trips to the well. We all hope for what we do not have—for who hopes for what they already have (Romans 8:24–25)? We hope for solutions to problems that won't go away; cures for the curses of modern life; resolution for our conflicts and reconciliation in relationships that drive us to the edge of sanity. We begin the journey to our wells in hope, even though we are in danger of being victims of hit-and-run accidents. The ongoing challenges of our lives do not abate, even while we are on the journey to the well. We may be hit hard and run over, pushed to the side like roadkill waiting for the appropriate agency to dispose of our bodies.

Like the Samaritan woman who is down to her last hope and has no one to turn to, we too can be moved by our one hope as we carry on with our responsibilities in the midst of trials; get ourselves to the well; and have transformational experiences with the Creator. In this chapter, as our hearts and minds are drawn into the world of this woman from Samaria, we will explore what it means to be down to our last things, our one last hope—in fact, sometimes holding on to the very idea of hope—then getting to the well, experiencing transformation, and, finally, celebrating the woman each of us is becoming, a woman of hope waiting patiently for what we do not have.

WHAT ARE YOUR LAST THINGS?

Have you ever been down to your last things? Have you ever realized your last something was in sight? You may not have planned it that way, but one day you looked up and discovered you were down to your last paycheck, last friend, last dream, last chance, last anything? Have you ever opened your wallet and discovered your last dollar or awakened one morning to open the dresser drawer and find your last pair of panty hose or clean underwear? And what about seeing that last piece of chicken in the refrigerator, or the last slice of pizza or cake? Have you ever been down to your last anything? Like your last gallon of gas in the car, last drop of coffee, last nerve—the same last nerve you have functioned on for at least the last five or ten years? What about the last time you saw his face, or the last time your family was all together? Most people don't want to think about the last song they'll ever sing or the last benediction they'll ever hear. And no one wants to think about the last minute, hour, or day when they'll pray that last prayer, see a last face before their eyes close to open no more, as they take their last breath.

Sometimes we're down to our last ounce of energy, our last surviving coping skill. We've all had bad days: completing an assignment with the flu, feeling disappointed and still getting up every morning to feed the children and get them to school on time, falling down emotionally and getting up the best you can as soon as you can, moving forward because the show must go on. How many times do we rise above our fears, problems, and circumstances to do the tasks assigned to us as women, and to us as people? We learn to work through colds, fever, depression, gossip, flu, divorce, separation, death of loved ones, and physical and emotional upheavals to complete assignments and responsibilities. Meanwhile, the one hope no one asks us about is being carried close to us, like the pot the Samaritan woman carries to Jacob's well. We carry our hopes around with us day in and day out. No one asks about our empty water pots, no one talks to us about our hopes, and frankly no one really cares. Sometimes we almost feel too tired to keep carrying those empty water pots. Sometimes it seems as though however much we do, the only things the people around us care about are: Did we get enough water for today, or did we cook dinner, clean the house, settle the children, type the report, check the e-mail, pay the bills, stop at the grocery store, the cleaners, or the video rental store? Did we make the beds, walk the dog, write the thank you note, clean up the mess, complete the presentation, and return the telephone calls? Did we do what we were supposed to do? Did we take care of business? Did we take care of their needs?

Even if you somehow do all that and feel you can organize your life in such a way as to leave no room for the unexpected, still, you may find one day that you of all people are down to your last something. You can store extras of everything tangible and create sophisticated backup systems only to discover that one day, in spite of all your efforts and investments you find yourself down to your last something. Some last things you may want in your life: paying the last mortgage payment, making the last car payment, being down to the last cigarette, or changing that last diaper. Last things can be both positive and negative. When they are positive they carry a sense of hope, but when they are negative it can be devastating.

When my mother died without warning on a sunny April Sunday afternoon, I felt all hope had left me. The one who had known me longer and better than anyone else in this world was no longer here for me. How was I going to carry on with life's responsibilities without her? My one hope was that I would somehow find the strength and the will to do what needed to be done. Mom and I had talked the night before and she had shared with me her thoughts about the annual conference we had just attended. She had attended every one since I had become a pastor in the early 1980s, and she always stood by my side, along with my husband, as I nervously reported on behalf of the people of whatever congregation I was serving at the time. She was always a supportive presence in the lives of my brother and me. Now she was gone without one last good-bye. I would not be able to say "I love you" one more time, not be able to hug her one more time; there would be no more sharing of secrets, confidante conversations, morning tea, or midnight chats. Every Monday morning, I had visited mother after dropping the children off at their schools or completing my early-morning shift at WEBB radio. It was a mother-and-daughter teatime of sharing. There were times, I admit, when panic took charge of life and mother would have to remind me to "Act first, panic later." At these times my mother would repeat my sermons back to me; preachers need to be preached to sometimes.

Now the one who knew me best was no longer active in my life. The one who observed all the transitions in my life was no longer visible—only her echoing words: Act first, panic later. But I could not act. I felt cheated that there were no lingering bedside chats, no role reversals, and no long good-byes. It was over; the present had become the future, and a future without my mother lay before me. Action was no longer a viable option and panic was in control, becoming the operative modality from which all decisions were made: the funeral arrangements, flowers, Omega service of her sorority, wake, influx of family, hosting and feeding guests, wills, social security, the cancellation of whatever was going on in our lives, and being strong for others. I was in danger of postponing the grief just to get through the day, promising myself, "Tomorrow I will deal with this unexpected upheaval in my life." I was in a state of panic, not faith. And there was more. A handful of seniors died in my congregation following my mother's death. For the next few months I was going from home to hospital to mortician to church to yet another grave site. At each death I relived my mother's passing with the family, crying with each remaining family member, grieving over each death as if it was my mother's. Finally, I told God I had had enough. How could I be there for someone else's family when I could barely be there for myself? How could I minister to someone else when I needed someone to minister to me? In the afterglow of memories, I again heard my mother's voice, "Act first, panic later."

I was in a wilderness just as dry as the barren desert sands that the

Samaritan woman journeyed through on that fateful day in Palestine. Her life was out of control. I too felt my life was beyond my control. What I thought I knew, I really didn't. What used to work was no longer working. Just as the Samaritan woman's one hope was that one day things would change, I now hoped that I would survive the latest change. Like the woman at the well, I felt that my life was out of control.

The Samaritan woman's life was out of control, but she also knew that she had to still take care of her own responsibilities. She was probably the city's "pass around girl"—every man got a turn. What she really needed to do was work on her life but she had to go to the well in order to survive. Water retrieval was a necessary task, a task that was generally assigned to women. Cities grew up around water sources, families came together or broke apart in disputes over water, and nations went to war, and will probably continue to do so, because of the value of water in a dry land. Water was needed for cooking, washing utensils and clothing, and for the planting, growing, and harvesting of crops. Water was needed to satisfy the parched dry throats of both humans and animals and to sustain life. Women were required to rise as early as necessary to retrieve the liquid resource that assured the continuation of life: It was a woman's job, her duty and responsibility, to get the water; no matter what was going on in her life she still had to fetch water on a daily basis.

The Samaritan woman was not the first woman in the Bible to wrestle with last things. The Old Testament book of 1 Kings 17 describes how the widow of Zarephath was down to her last ounce of oil and her last grains of meal. She cared for herself since she had no husband or grown son to provide for her. She was resigned to the fact that she had reached the bottom of the barrel. A famine plagued her land; a famine that the prophet Elijah had predicted to King Ahab. A drought would occur that would last about three and one-half years. This meant there would be no rain, no planting, and no harvest to replenish her food supply, and so she planned to fix her last meal with the remaining oil and die. Last things for her meant death because she had stopped seeking answers. When faced with her last things, she did not even hope for the unexpected or for Divine intervention.

The prophet Elijah knew something about last things too. When he was obedient to Yahweh and predicted a famine, he was rewarded with the anger of King Ahab and forced to flee the king's control. He was beyond King Ahab's jurisdiction but he was not beyond the provisions of God. While Elijah stayed in the Transjordan at a brook called Cherith, God commanded the ravens to feed him twice daily. Every day Elijah was down to his last meal, and twice daily he was down to his last supply of food. Every day, twice a day, God provided just what Elijah needed to survive. When the brook dried up, God sent Elijah to the widow of Zarephath to be fed, but she herself was down to her last oil and meal. It is often in the midst of last things that we are able to see the handiwork of God and find a provision that can only be attributed to God, not to intellect, education, employment, family, or friend. It is at our dried-up brooks and streams where we learn that God can still do more than we asked for (Ephesians 3:20). When Elijah faced that last meal and last trickle of water flowing through the brook at Cherith, God's voice directed him to a woman who was wrestling with *her* last things. "Go at once to Zarephath of Sidon and stay there. I have commanded a widow in that place to supply you with food" (1 Kings 17:9). God didn't mention famine or lack of food. Surely this Yahweh, the God that had been faithful to Elijah for nearly one year, feeding him with the help of food-bearing ravens, would continue to be faithful again as he joined this widow who was down to own her last meal. When the prophet Elijah arrived he asked her to prepare him a meal from her last supply of oil and meal. For her this meant that the last things would not be for her own personal consumption, and naturally the widow resisted by stating her lack of provision. But Elijah persuaded her to first fix him a cake, and then to make a meal for herself and her young son. He assured her that God would not allow her supply of meal and oil to run out until God returned rain to the land (1 Kings 17:14). The widow made the cake and served it to the prophet, and as she kept making meals and giving away her last things she discovered that *what was supposed to run out did not.* She had enough for herself, her son, and the prophet. God had met all of their needs with her last things.

There are similarities between the widow of Zarephath and the woman at the well. The names of both women are lost in antiquity and they are identified only by their location: one in Zarephath in Sidon and the other by a well near Sychar. The widow was a Gentile and the woman at the well was a Samaritan—both were considered outside the covenant of God, yet both were instruments used by God to save or assist others. The widow was used to sustain the prophet Elijah; the woman at the well was used to ignite a revival in Sychar. The prophet Elijah interrupted the widow's famine, in the same way Jesus the Christ of Nazareth interrupted the spiritual famine of the Samaritan woman and her community. God took what the widow had and multiplied it; Jesus took the woman at the well and transformed her. The widow of Zarephath was down to her last things and so was the woman at the well. The widow was down to her last oil and meal; the woman at the well was down to her last hope, her last chance, and at the last place she wanted to see someone: Jacob's well outside of Sychar.

No one bothered to ask the Samaritan woman about her hopes as she carried her one hope with her to the well. It was her last hope. She had to get to the well! She didn't know it yet, but it was her last hope that would change things. She came to the well one day to get water and her life was never the same again. Jesus was at the well, and he offered her water that was filling and satisfying. She had left the city to escape the gossip of those who talked about her less-than-perfect lifestyle, those who participated in her relationship roulette. She was a woman who was passed around to five different men and was living with another outside the legal and cultural tradition of marriage. It was a less than perfect relationship, outside the laws of the community. It was a scandal in her generation, and eyebrows would still be raised in ours. Her lifestyle created an atmosphere where she was uncomfortable with herself and others were uncomfortable with her. But the Samaritan woman returned to the city a new woman, not motivated by her physical needs, but by a spiritual relationship with Jesus Christ. She returned to the city after encountering more than just a man. Jesus only demanded water, but he gave her what every woman wants in life: to belong, to be accepted, and to be valued.

TRANSFORMATION THROUGH LIVING WATER

When you're stuck in the desert of life and water is running low or you're out of water or need fresh water, get to the well. Jesus will meet you there. Hold on to hope! Faith requires us to hold on to our hopes, not our fears. Everyone has fears, but they have different names: loneliness, abandonment, low self-esteem, addictions, emptiness, health issues, grief, longing, identity crises, stagnation, unhealthy habits, unhealthy relationships, or pain. Jesus met the woman at the well in the same way the angel of the Lord met Hagar during her desert experience (Genesis 21). Hagar was down to her last hope. Abraham and Sarah had forced her out of their home. This single parent was forced into the wilderness without any job referrals, homeless shelters, food stamps, or marketable skills. She was down to her last drop of water. Hagar put her son under a bush and sat down, crying, not wanting to see him die. Hold on to your last hope!

God heard her cries. God opened her eyes, and she saw a well of water. God then promised to make her son, Ishmael, the leader of a great and mighty nation. Hagar kept going in an unfamiliar, unforgiving environment while trying to perform her parental responsibilities. Fear blinded her eyes so she couldn't see help right in front of her. Why begin the journey in fear? Fear may change or taint the outcome. Hope opens your eyes to the resources that fear refuses to see. Fear loses its grip through the process of transformation discovered in the story of the woman at the well. We can all join her in this journey to the well.

When I was down to the last minutes of labor on the highway, fear said I wouldn't make it. Hope said to keep going. Hold on, you will get to the well. In this case, I got to the hospital, where help was waiting for me. As I was rolled through the hospital doors, only moments later giving birth, my one hope became reality. Labor pains are not fun, but nature, along with the doctors and nurses, transformed my pain into joy. The miracle of life—birth—is a transformative, miraculous moment for everyone involved! I had made it to the well.

"In the year that King Uzziah died, I saw the Lord . . ." (Isaiah 6:1). In the year my mother died, I had a new encounter with Jesus at a well of reflection, refreshment, and renewal that set the stage for transformation. In my spiritual wilderness the voice of the Lord spoke over the wail of panic and pain. I had the legacy my mother left me, but what I really wanted was to hear her voice one more time. Instead I heard the voice of Jesus, "Though my father and mother forsake me, the Lord will receive me" (Psalm 27:10). I now had these new words to hold on to. It is not that my mother's words were invalid—they had sustained me in times past, but the Words of Christ held me even when my mother's words couldn't reach me. This was water for my soul, the very life-giving, healing Word of God. I had known it was there—how could I not know that? Still, panic had choked the desire to put God's Word into action.

Every year, I preach the women's week of services at Trinity United Church of Christ in Chicago, Illinois. Dr. Jeremiah Wright, a pastor's pastor, mentor, brother, and friend invites me to preach eight times in six days during women's week. The year my mother died, I almost didn't go to Trinity. Remember—panic was in control. At the last minute, I decided not to cancel and to preach through the storm. As I prayed and searched the scriptures in preparation for the sermons I would preach, my eye caught this story of the woman at the well in the Gospel of John, chapter four. As a preacher, you can either preach your observation about a text; share the historical setting and social relevance; or you can step inside the text and allow its power to work on you as you devour its contents to your soul's edification, thereby allowing the power of the text to work through you to the edification of those who sit at the foot of the cross listening. Preaching is a transparent moment. Humanity must become invisible so that divinity becomes crystal clear. If anyone needed an encounter with the Divine in a desert place I did. I preached the series of eight sermons in six days to over 2,500 people each night, and at the time I felt I was there for them. In retrospect, God was taking me through the process of transformation, while at the same time ministering to those in the congregation. In order to write those texts I had to become honest and intimate with my grief and with myself. It was a transforming experience. In order to walk in the Samaritan woman's footsteps you must become honest and intimate with yourself.

We are all women with one hope. We can become women of hope, celebrating when our one hope becomes a reality, whether it is a successful birth or death with dignity, while waiting patiently for things to change. Who hopes for what she already has?

CELEBRATE THE WOMAN OF HOPE YOU ARE BECOMING

Like the Samaritan woman at the well, we all shoulder our water-toting responsibilities and make the necessary trips to the well. We fight through our fears one step at a time. We're searching for the substance to sustain our hopes: the hope that one day, things will change.

I experienced the Divine that Sunday when my one hope to deliver my child with the doctor and hospital I knew was fulfilled. We made it to the hospital and did we ever celebrate. There is a God, and God cared that I had one hope that day. How appropriate that my one hope came to fruition as the Bethel congregation I'd been serving celebrated women's day!

My mother celebrated life up until the last minute. She had been attending a women's convention sponsored by a local radio station at the Baltimore Convention Center. A journalist to the end, she'd just finished interviewing a singing group and was leaving to get dinner. She collapsed and died doing what she loved, not home alone as she had feared, or after lingering long in a nursing home. She died in the midst of a crowd, working and celebrating life; that had been her one hope.

CALL TO ACTION

Journey to the Well is more than an attempt to interpret the biblical text; rather, it is the telling of the story from the Samaritan woman's side of the page as she emerges as a significant part of the salvation plan of God. She is no longer lost in his story, but now has a story of her own. Many women have been wounded by poor decisions; decisions they made and decisions others made for them. They have been forced to retreat because they cannot connect with their sisters, shrouded by the must-dos of their own lives. We can see ourselves reflected in her journey, trudging through the necessary task of water retrieval, hesitating at the unexpected intruder who shatters our anonymity, exposing our vulnerabilities at the well. We are shocked when he ignores cultural taboos and speaks to us. We identify with her probing questions, and we duck and dodge disclosing our own intimacies.

As we make our journey out of our limitations—habitual, historical, and cultural—toward what we will come to know as our Created Purpose, we pause to reflect upon our past mistakes. If all you have is a little bit, make the most of it. If all you have is a dream, hold on to your dream. If all you have is one hope, hold on. If all you have is broken pieces, gather them up and hold on until your dream comes true. If all you have is an idea, nurture it. If all you have is a rope, tie a knot in it and hold on. And if all you have is one well outside of town, get to it. Open your eyes to see the Jesus who was there all along in the ordinary places of your life. Take your one hope and your last things and become a woman of hope. Begin now to celebrate the woman you are becoming, a woman of hope.

Discipline of the Well

Well Lessons

The first lesson of the well is that when we get down to our last anything, thinking there is nothing left, when we think that the last thing, last nerve, last drop of water, last dollar is all gone, over—hold on. Being down to your last things can lead to something unexpected happening. Hagar, the widow of Zarephath, Elijah, the woman at the well: All were down to their last things and something unexpectedly happened that changed their situations when they thought all hope was gone. There was Divine intervention. God responded to their plights. Hope triumphed and fear was defeated.

Women of hope know that last things can lead to something happening. Last things are never the final answer. Hope can triumph, and fear can be the weakest link. Good-bye! Women of hope know that last things can be the prelude to new beginnings.

The second lesson is that God can change your situation and that God can change you. The Samaritan woman's story is a story of personal transformation. Her situation remained the same, but she was changed by the encounter. Women of hope must be willing to become intimate with themselves and with God. They must be open to new realities, not only within their situations, but within themselves. The one hope that things will change may actually be the hope that one day I will change!

The third lesson is learning to celebrate one hope at a time. The authentic experience of the journey to our own wells may take a few hours, days, weeks, months, or years. Celebrate along the way.

When one of our children turned sixteen, she turned her birthday into a monthlong celebration: a luncheon with classmates, a party at school, a big fete at home with a DJ, a sleepover. She had long lists of ways to prolong the festivities and the receiving of gifts.

Women of hope: You have begun your journeys to the well. Begin to celebrate each step. Every time fear is defeated, celebrate. Every time panic is put down, dread dies, or tears of mourning are turned into shouts of joy, celebrate. Celebrate each step taken through fear to do what needs to be done.

On the mantelpiece of our home we have a drawing of my grandfather. It shows him lighting a candle in the dark. The glow of the candle illuminates his face and the space around him. That's what hope does. It lights a candle in the darkness. Fear may try to blow it out, but women of hope are learning how to carry an extra pack of matches. Celebrate that woman we will need to become to begin this journey, as women of hope.

Well Words

"For I know the plans I have for you," declares the Lord, "plans to prosper you and not to harm you, plans to give you hope and a future." .

JEREMIAH 29:11

Now faith is being sure of what we hope for and certain of what we do not see.

HEBREWS 11:1

. . . but those who hope in the Lord will renew their strength.

ISAIAH 40:31

Put your hope in God, for I will yet praise him, my Savior . . .

PSALM 42:5

We have this hope as an anchor for the soul, firm and secure.

HEBREWS 6:19

Be joyful in hope, patient in affliction, faithful in prayer.

Well Sabbatical

⟶ *Write in your travel log or journal about a time when you had only one hope.*

⟶ *Write about a time you were down to your last something.*

⟶ *Spend five minutes meditating on the hymn "My Hope Is Built on Nothing Less."*

My Hope Is Built on Nothing Less

*My hope is built on nothing less than Jesus' blood and righteous-
ness;*
I dare not trust the sweetest frame, but wholly lean on Jesus' name.
*His oath, His covenant, . . . His blood support me in the over-
whelming flood;*
*When all around my soul gives way, He then is all my hope and
stay.*
On Christ the solid rock, I . . . stand.
All other ground is sinking sand, All other ground is sinking sand.

(AME HYMNAL, P. 364. WORDS: EDWARD MOTE;
MUSIC: WILLIAM B. BRADBURY)

Well Language

⟶ *One day things will change.*

⟶ *Hope is the key that unlocks the door.*

⌒ *If I have hope, I have help.*

⌒ *If you have hope, you have help.*

⌒ *With God, nothing is impossible.*

⌒ *I am confident in the name of Jesus Christ.*

⌒ *I am capable of doing all things through Christ, who strengthens me.*

⌒ *Because of Christ, I am confident that I can respond to knowledge, information, events, and challenge in my life.*

⌒ *Carry on, you can make it!*

Well Work

1. *Make a list of your own last things.*
2. *Read 1 Kings 17.*
3. *Start your collage. Select your surface: large board, poster board, cork, canvas, bulletin board, a wall, or a large drawing pad. Be creative! Collect images and objects that remind you of your one hope, and mount them on your collage surface.*
4. *Write in your journal about when you were down to your last things. Also write about what is the one thing you are hoping for now.*

2

A Woman Open to God

Now he had to go through Samaria.

JOHN 4:4

Susan had been wrestling with tough family issues for months. She prayed, fasted, and consulted spiritual mentors, counselors, and friends. She went from revivals to church conferences to special events with out-of-town speakers. She read books and amassed a great video and cassette library. Susan was listening for God to speak to her at these events and through experts and friends. One day while reading the Bible in her personal time, she came across Psalm 46:10. "Be still, and know that I am God." Susan left her bedroom and sat on the front steps of her city home, watching kids play ball in the street as an older man, one she'd not seen before, coached the boys. The man was giving the kids pointers on how to win the game. It seemed to Susan that what the man was saying to the boys was just what she needed to hear to help her with her own young son. The man said, "All I am is the coach who gives you the plays to run. It is up to you to run the plays without being distracted, while looking for unexpected opportunities to advance the ball."

Susan sat still listening with her spirit. The Word of God is better than the NFL playbook of Super Bowl champions in the game of life. Her Divine Creator was the coach and the Bible was the playbook. Live the

Word without being distracted and look for unexpected opportunities to advance.

This did not occur in a grand cataclysmic event but within the ordinary weave of the everyday. God is able to meet us in both the ordinary and the extraordinary and to coach us from the sidelines.

Jesus came to the Samaritan woman while she was performing the most ordinary task: going to the well. Think of the Samaritan woman in ancient times, at a desert well, looking for the water she needed to survive. It doesn't get much more basic than that. Much of life is ordinary; that's exactly where God meets us—in the ordinary. We keep looking for the special moment, the big bang, the wow, the extraordinary, and the magical, when all the time our Redeemer is available to us at ordinary times and in ordinary places. We often rush past our moments in life to keep pace with the chores assigned to us, so focused on the technicalities of running the plays, we miss the unexpected opportunity to advance. We miss the moment we're living in.

Like the Samaritan woman meeting God in the ordinary, we too can be open to God in everyday events as we discover our destiny with the Creator and connect with others. In this chapter we will become women of unexpected opportunities as we discover ways God has of speaking to us. If we listen, we'll discern that he is present with us every day in the everyday moments, that he will find us in our out-of-the-ordinary hiding places if we try to avoid Him, that we can be open to God and take action to reach out. What kinds of ordinary places will God meet you in?

GOD MEETS US IN THE ORDINARY

God in the ordinary? Ordinary is so everyday, so routine, without any of the special pizzazz associated with a particular event or experience. We all have everyday clothes, everyday shoes, everyday dishes with everyday meals, everyday linens and towels, and everyday activities. We do everyday work in and outside the home. We wear our everyday hair-styles with our everyday suits and dresses to our regular, everyday jobs. We watch our everyday television shows, listen to the radio in the car on the way to work every day. Every day we take in and eliminate; our blood flows, hearts beat, and lungs expand and contract. The sun breaks over the horizon without invitation, and even if you want the day to start earlier or later, it cannot because it arrives every day as the Earth spins on its axis in its orbit around the sun. It rises without your permission, input, or energy. It comes every day; it goes every day. You may want to hold on to the day, but every day will end when the sun sinks below the horizon, *every day*. Who would expect the God who created it all to still be present in the ordinary every day?

I remember thinking one time that I couldn't wait until my children were out of diapers. Then it was walking, or in school, or driving, or out of college, or living on their own. I was in one moment of their lives forever looking to the next. Finally, I realized I was missing all my ordinary moments with them, moments that can never be relived. Enjoy the ordinary and you'll see God visits you there as well, take the time to listen to the wind and hear God, enjoy a moment of silence and hear the Creator whisper to you in a still small voice, find the Divine in your regular routine.

There was a time when I used to envy male pastors who could close their study doors and write sermons in undisturbed quiet. Their spouses would keep the children quiet, the house quiet, and take the phone messages until the prophet emerged with Sunday's word. I learned to hear God while changing diapers, washing dishes, bandaging cuts and bruises, settling sibling disputes, and fixing meals. God met me in my ordinary moments and transformed the ordinary with the essence of his presence and divinity. The kitchen became a sanctuary, the dining room table became a tabernacle, and the office became the altar upon which the sacrifice of praise was made.

Who would expect that a God who heals, delivers, and blesses would take precious time to visit the ordinary? Why would a God so holy step into the ordinary and help those who are struggling? Why did Jesus stop for an ordinary Samaritan woman? Let me remind you that this is the same God who sent His son, the King of Kings and Lord of Lords, to an ordinary young teenage virgin who rode an ordinary donkey to Bethlehem with her espoused, Joseph, an ordinary carpenter. That son was born in an ordinary stable, wrapped in ordinary cloth, laid in a trough where animals ate ordinary straw on the floor, far away from the extraordinary palaces of earthly kings. This is the God who walked in the cool of the evening in a garden looking for Adam. The God who spoke to Moses from a burning bush, who stopped Paul on a Damascus road, who slept in a boat in the middle of the storm, who was criticized for eating with sinners and wine drinkers; who talked to Samaritan women, blind men, lepers, and a widow on the way to bury her only son. So it was in an ordinary moment, getting water, that Jesus met the Samaritan woman. They met in the most ordinary and basic of places, a life-giving well.

It is ingenious of Christ to begin the Samaritan woman's personal transformation with the object she first came to know in life. Her life first began in the embryonic waters of her mother's womb. She would be born again not through these waters, but through Living Water offered by Christ when he decided to pin his theological discussion on water at the well. It is a simple, yet complex, element. Marisa Fox writes that we have always looked to water for healing (O, *the Oprah Magazine*, June 2001, pp. 170–74). The Romans built elaborate aqueducts to bring water to soak in to their nine hundred bathhouses. Cleopatra bathed in it. Tolstoy and Mozart spent time in spas immersed in water; health practitioners encourage us to drink eight glasses a day of it. Thousands of vacationers drive hundreds of miles to sit by it. Millions of tapes, records, and CDs are sold so that people can hear it as rain gently falling or waves crashing violently against a rocky shore. Water is the first environment that we all come to know. We are surrounded by the sound of water as our cells multiply and divide according to an amazing plan embedded in our DNA. The first sound we hear is filtered through water. The first movements we make are in water. The first knowledge of life comes to us from ordinary, life-giving water.

The Samaritan woman came to the well, an ordinary place. The last place you expect to find this all-powerful, all-knowing God is in the ordinary. You'd expect to find God among the celestial aristocracy, high and lifted upon a throne, with the stars of the universe configured in a royal arch of triumph, angels singing praises in eternity at the Lord's beck and call. Any and every occasion can be an encounter with the Divine. The difference between this Samaritan woman on her way to the well and us is that our journey is made with expectations. She did not expect anything beyond the ordinary.

GOD WILL FIND YOU IN OUT-OF-THE-ORDINARY WAYS

God is there, even if we are hiding out like the Samaritan woman was as she moved steadily in the noonday sun, wrapped in the multilayered garments of her time, carrying her empty pots to draw water from the well. It was high noon, the sixth hour of the Jewish day, which runs from six A.M. to six P.M. Most women came to the well for water at two different times, either early in the morning while temperatures were cool or in the evening just when the sun was sinking below the horizon. A woman at the well at the hottest hour of the day was unusual, as only women who *had* to come came at that hour. Only women who wanted to avoid the stares and talk of townspeople came to the well at high noon. Women who had something to hide came to the well at the hottest hour of the day.

Put yourself in her place. You're trying to avoid people, and you see a guy standing by the well, even though you've taken all this trouble to arrive when you're sure no one will be there. You may even slow your approach, trying to assess by studying his clothes or demeanor whether this man is friend or foe. We have only just begun our discussion of the journey to the well and already we have discovered an anonymous woman sneaking to the well at the wrong time of day. Without knowing anything else about her, her timing alone suggests a suspicious lifestyle. She is convicted by circumstantial evidence based on being in the wrong place at the wrong time. Things were so bad in her world that she left the city to draw water from a suburban well, located about one-half mile from Sychar. She left the cisterns in her community to hike on hot, dusty roads to draw water from the well, forced to go to the only place she could get what she needed. This is an anonymous woman who knows how to disappear while all the other women are focused on other activities. The ancient text can tell us what she said, but it does not reveal her attitude. There is no hint whether or not she was annoyed that someone else was at the well that day and no indication that she was disturbed that someone saw her at the well. We only know that she was a woman with one hope at one well and Jesus was waiting for her to arrive.

The woman at the well reminds me of a woman I knew. Cheryl had begun avoiding the world around her because she felt inadequate. She had become like wallpaper, unobtrusively decorating the walls of everyone's life including her own, covering surfaces without ever being noticed. She preferred it that way, especially when she was asked to volunteer in her community. Remembering that she had been rather effective in college using her volunteer skills, Cheryl imagined what her world might be like if things changed. She really did want to feel that she belonged in the community, but she reasoned that she wouldn't be good enough; besides, her time and heart were set on other priorities. Whenever someone approached her about volunteering, all she wanted to do was disappear from his or her radar screen for a few stolen, solitary moments at the well. She just wanted to fade to black in the middle of her own movie. Cheryl no longer wanted to be a visible part of her community.

It is amazing that the more we try to disappear, the more visible we become to the Divine. Jesus has a way of noticing every detail of the universe; even the fringes, margins, wallpapers, backgrounds, and the hiding places of disappearing, anonymous women, like Cheryl and the Samaritan woman, are visible to him. The more we try to disappear, the more we appear to Him.

To understand fully just how clearly Jesus sees invisible women like the Samaritan woman and how far He goes to find them, it is helpful to think about the Book of John, the book in which we find the story of the Samaritan woman, and also to think about the context of what was occurring around Jesus at this time. John gives us a Gospel that pulls together the sayings of Jesus and intertwines them with narrative, dialogue, and discourse. The purpose is to lead readers to know that Jesus is the Christ, the Son of God, and that by believing in Him, we may have life in his name (John 20:31). Matthew, Mark, and Luke, in the Synoptic Gospels, focus mostly on the ministry of Jesus in Galilee. Matthew wants readers to know Jesus as the Son of David, Mark portrays Jesus as the Son of God, and Luke shows us Jesus as the universal Savior. Their messages are quite similar. John, on the other hand, wants readers to know Jesus, to know that He is the Son of God, the eternal Word that was in the beginning, that He was with God, and is God (John 1:1-5). Jesus is the Logos or the Word made into flesh, and He dwelt among us (John 1:14).

Water was crucially important in this desert area, and John uses images of water as he writes his Gospel. In John's chapter two, Jesus turns water into wine at the wedding in Cana. In chapter three, Jesus tells the rabbi Nicodemus, "Except a man be born of water and of the Spirit, he cannot enter into the kingdom of Heaven." Christ goes on to Judea, then, where John the Baptist was baptizing people. Religious leaders in Judea criticized Jesus for baptizing more disciples than John the Baptist had baptized. In fact, it was actually Jesus' disciples who were baptizing people. Because of the local leaders' criticism, Jesus decided to avoid the controversy concerning the baptisms by leaving Judea and going north to Galilee. The fastest way north from Judea was through Samaria. It was the fastest, but also the most dangerous, not because of the terrain, but because of the hostilities between the Jews and the Samaritans. The longest and safest way was to go across the southern end of the Jordan River and proceed north up the far eastern side around Samaria. To enter Galilee, Jesus would then have to recross the Jordan River in the north. It would take twice as long to go around Samaria as it would to go through it.

To the casual observer this appears to be a chance meeting at Jacob's well. However, under close examination, this was a chance meeting *on purpose*. The biblical text indicates that it was necessary for Jesus to go through Samaria. "Now he had to go through Samaria" (John 4:4). Why? Was Jesus in a hurry? Was he pressed for time? Was there something or someone in Galilee that needed his immediate attention? Or was this an on-purpose meeting with an unsuspecting Samaritan woman at Jacob's well, an accident on purpose, and a destined, Divine coincidence?

Jesus chose the shortest way to Galilee—through Samaria—which could potentially put His life in danger. The Samaritans and Jews usually had no dealings with each other. The schism could be traced back to when the Assyrians captured Shechem at the foot of Mount Gerizim in 722 B.C. Most of the people of Israel were carried away to Assyria, and those Jews who remained during the occupation intermarried with other ethnic groups in the land. The Jerusalem Jews to the south of Judah looked upon them with disdain and believed the mixed marriages were against God's law. The Samaritans, as they came to be called, worshiped the same God and they believed in the first five books of the Jewish Bible, or what Christians call the first five books in the Old Testament. Yet Jews and Samaritans would not share a meal or pass a fork across a table. Encounters between them were often violent and bitter, a real old-fashioned Hatfield and McCoy family feud. Hatred between them increased when the Samaritans' offer to help rebuild the Jerusalem temple was refused because of the intermarrying. Some Samaritans decided to hinder the effort to rebuild the temple since their help had been refused. This occurred nearly seventy years after the Babylonian captivity.

The Samaritans built their own temple on Mount Gerizim. They consider this mount, rather than Jerusalem, the central place of worship, and to this day they still sacrifice the Passover lamb on Mount Gerizim. Because of this, there was great animosity between the Jews and the Samaritans. It was remarkable that Jesus decided to go through Samaria rather than around it. Samaritans would, upon occasion, take their anger out on the Jews who were walking in the area. If a Jew was caught in Samaria, he could be beaten up and abused. If a Samaritan somehow lost his way and got caught in Hebrew territory, the same thing could happen to him. It was good to know and stay on your own turf.

Rather than avoid a dangerous encounter with a hated and despised people, Jesus made a decision to go through Samaria. Now, against all good reason, Jesus was in Samaria. This was no chance meeting; there are no chance meetings with God. This meeting was no fluke; it was no accident. Jesus had to go. So He intentionally went through hostile territory to see a woman who was down to her last things at Jacob's well, a woman with only one last hope.

Just the idea that God would take a detour is an exhilarating thought. Could it be that what we think of as all the coincidences in our lives are not really coincidences? Could it be that those chance meetings, chance conversations, chance activities, may not have been so chancy after all? A Redeemer leaves the crowd to search out the individual just like a shepherd leaves the flock of ninety-nine to seek out the one stray lost lamb, or the Savior makes house calls when friends are ill. When a Messiah pauses in his journey to pull children onto his lap, or heal a blind man's eyes, you want to become a woman of unexpected opportunities and to look up from your last things with the expectation that surely God is on the way.

BE OPEN TO GOD, ALWAYS

Everyone at Sydney's place of employment felt that she was just plain lucky, but she knew differently. While driving home from work on the freeway, Sydney was listening to gospel music and quietly praying about family issues. As she stilled herself in prayer to hear from God, praising, confessing, and believing, she distinctly heard a voice telling her to turn off and go home another way. Sydney had been sensitive to the still, small voice of God that often urged her to change directions, change her mind, change her course of action, and she responded even though it sounded like an odd request to leave a freeway at rush hour. What Sydney didn't know was that soon police officers would be chasing a car on that freeway—a car whose occupants were shooting at each other. Innocent people were shot along the way, one died. Because she was open to the voice of God and God's new marching order, Sydney was kept out of harm's way.

Being open to God is not limiting God with your own preconceived notions or your idea of the future. Being open to God is not shackling God with what you want, how you feel, where you want to be, and what you deserve to be doing right now. It is giving God a blank check and letting the Divine fill it in, trusting Him not to take more than necessary. Being open is telling God "I trust You with who I am and everything that I have." It is removing yourself from the control panel of your life, letting God drive, and not limiting God or putting God in your own narrow box.

As I struggled with the decision to go into full-time ministry, I was torn by my desire to continue my career in radio broadcasting. I wanted to go as far in broadcasting as I could before becoming a pastor of a congregation. I prayed and asked God which course of action to take: stay with my responsibilities at the radio station or devote all of my energies to a pastorate? I finally stopped praying about the two and simply asked God, "What do you want me to do? How do you want me to serve you?" I was willing to trust God for the answer and accept God's decision in the matter. What is the point of asking God for guidance if when an answer is finally given you set parameters for God to work around? "Lord, I want to do what You want me to do, but check with me first so I can approve of what You want from me." "Lord, I want to go where You want me to go, but check with me first about any change in destination or location." "Lord, whatever You decide is all right with me. My life is in Your hands, as long as I approve." Being open to God means not limiting the Lord with prerequisites, stipulations, or prearranged or preagreed decisions; you are open to suggestions and you are sensitive to them. Think of Job. He had it all going for him. He had a wife, many children, wealth, and a reputation for being an upright man. Even God bragged about Job. Behind the scenes God gave permission for Satan to mess with Job's life, sparing only his soul. One by one the material and physical aspects of Job's life fell apart. His three friends misinterpreted these events as evidence of Job's secret sin; they didn't see God as a silent player in the events of Job's life.

If God closes a door, then so be it. If God opens a door in an unexpected location, go for it. You take advantage of whatever God offers, whenever God offers, and the way God offers. Remember, run the plays looking for unexpected opportunities to advance. You are becoming a woman of unexpected opportunities. How easily we lose our sense of adventure. We leave wonderment behind in childhood and pick up routine as a habit in our maturity. During college, a girlfriend and I would declare every time we climbed into my mother's old white Valiant, "We're off on another adventure." We never went anywhere extravagant, yet we often drove caution crazy. We would leave our college campus not on a reckless journey, but just doing the ordinary tasks of life. It wasn't our destination that was exciting, but our attitude about going. We went looking for the unexpected to happen amidst the expected, and it always did. We stayed long enough to touch our environment and allow what we saw to touch us.

Have you ever been touched by a sunset? Have you ever been touched by a waterfall? Have you ever been touched by rolling, emerald green hills that tower above deep, lush valleys? Have you ever been touched by waves that give themselves to crashing upon the shore? Have you ever been touched by young girls playing double Dutch? Or touched by a little kid shooting marbles in the alley? Have you ever been touched by freshly mown grass on a spring day? Too often we are swept so quickly by the world of to-dos that we never allow anything or anyone to touch us. It is possible to learn lessons from the mundane, opening our senses to become one with the environment, taking the time to sense, to see what is not so readily revealed, to hear what has not been spoken, only whispered to the cosmos. Are you prepared to receive? If you are not careful you may become jealous of the Samaritan woman's journey. Thou shall not covet another woman's journey. Thou shalt have thine own journey.

When Cheryl finally opened up to those in her community she began to feel she was a part of the community. Her confidence level rose and pretty soon she wasn't hiding out any more. She started accepting invitations and used her skills and talents to do volunteer work with people she enjoyed. She had never felt so alive!

The Samaritan woman found out about miracles that day at Jacob's well. On the surface, this was just an ordinary day in the semiarid desert not too far from Mount Gerizim and the Samaritan city of Sychar; just a chance meeting at Jacob's well between a Jewish rabbi and a woman down to her last hope. Because the Samaritan woman was open to Jesus, a Jew in Samaria, she heard the Word of God.

Being open to God involves several of the senses including listening, seeing, and feeling within life's experiences. It is hearing God's voice in the whisper of the wind as it traces the curves of your face, gently slipping over your character lines and lingering long enough to be more than a breeze, becoming a whisper from heaven. Being open to God is listening to God; it is receiving a revelation that engages the mind, captures the heart, and encourages the soul. Like Sydney's rerouting her journey home by taking a different exit, it means being willing to do something because you're feeling led to do it. It is hearing, not quite fully understanding, yet confident that all will be made clear in the fullness of time. Being open to God is seeing the fingerprints of God on events and experience as evidence of Divine intervention; knowing that they were not coincidences, accidents, or easily explained occurrences because God was the unseen conductor of orchestrated events.

REACH OUT, CONNECT TO OTHERS

In ancient literature, sacred to both the church and the synagogue, at times writers have failed to record and witnesses have failed to remember personal details of many women. A woman comes to the well with one hope, but no name, no parental references, no communal notation, just the distinction of being Samaritan and female. The Bible is filled with countless women, many of them unnamed, their histories missing and significant genealogies absent. While pertinent information is given about others, for these women there is nothing. We know that Elijah was known as the Tishbite, resided in Gilead, and was perhaps born in Tishbe of Naphtali. We know that James and John were the sons of Zebedee; Joshua was the son of Nun; Lazarus was from Bethany and had two sisters named Mary and Martha; Aaron was a Levite, the brother of Moses and Miriam, the child of Abram and Jochebed. Women may be listed by location, such as the widow of Zarephath, widow of Nain, Queen of Sheba, or the wise woman of Takoa. Some women are referred to by circumstance: the woman caught in adultery or the woman with an issue of blood. At times women are listed simply as women. Luke records nameless personalities who were included because they could not be excluded (Luke 8:3 and 24:10). Their significance to God, the plan of salvation, or as instruments of the Divine, necessitated their inclusion, but the Holy Spirit did not require the lost and forgotten pieces of information for the telling of the story.

Perhaps one of the reasons we don't know the Samaritan woman's name is that she wanted to remain anonymous. Anonymous women live without acknowledgment; they don't want to be recognized so they unplug, disconnect, and withdraw from the community. They have learned how to disappear, be invisible on the job, in the neighborhood, and even in their own homes, blending into the background of life. Anonymous women are everywhere, you just don't notice them; they are present, remaining faceless in a crowd. You meet them and can never remember their names because they've learned to hide distinguishing characteristics like a Klingon vessel hides behind a cloaking device.

In 1985, the Circle of Love was born out of a shared experience in a congregation I was serving as pastor. It was a women's Bible fellowship where we each sought Godly answers to our daily dilemmas, as part of a secure environment in a healing community for sharing the one hope, the last things, and the situations that separated us from community and Christ. The rules were simple: Any woman could attend. Membership in the church was not required. What was shared in the Circle stayed in the Circle; we believed that some things were best shared comfortably within a sisterhood and that nothing would be discussed or disclosed outside the Circle. No one would sit in condemnation or be judged. Women who were not members of the congregation were invited to tell their stories within the Circle of Love. Many of these women had tasted the bittersweet chocolate side of life; it may have been chocolate, but it was still bitter to the taste. They had been through trials and had emerged triumphant on the other side. Women told stories of rape on a date, incest with a parent, divorce, abortion, and miscarriage; they shared their frustrations with family issues, empty nests, migraines, depression, foreclosures, relocation, procrastination, retirement, menopause, money problems, harassment, misplaced hopes, and lost dreams. Miracles happened in the Circle of Love. Women found the strength to tell their own stories and search for answers. They learned from one another's experiences, and those with similar experiences bonded when they found someone who understood what they were going through. Women went back to school, opened businesses, came out of hiding, found out they were not alone, refused to be anonymous, reconnected, stayed sane, and found themselves and Christ at the Circle of Love. They found out that dreams do come true and miracles still happen.

* * *

Only those who intentionally look for wallpaper women and background women locate them on the fringes of existence. One of the members of our congregation uses her Sunday bulletin to reach out to people who won't reach out on their own. She selects a person on the bus and subway routes she travels daily to and from work, gives them the bulletin, asking simply that they enjoy some of the activities. She smiles, and she invites them to join her. Another friend uses audiotaped copies of the Sunday sermon to share with women in her neighborhood and family, sometimes even mailing them to people all across the country. She may know them, or she may have met them during her travels. An excellent way to reach out to those who live in the margins of our community is to take Sunday bulletins, favorite audio- and video-tapes, magazines, and books to share at nursing homes, hospitals, hospices, and support groups. Read or play the tapes where you can, bring toys and school supplies to children, volunteer at a soup kitchen, take toiletries and personal items to a homeless shelter, or be a hugger at a Special Olympics event. There is an invisible woman in every group. Make it a point to include her in your activities. Be patient with those who still shy away from center stage and give them time to begin to identify themselves apart from the background. Many senior women withdraw from active life when their bodies slow down and health begins to fail. They become a part of the background when lifelong friends and spouses precede them in death, or their adult children may not give them a place in their lives due to personal decisions, busy vocations, or because they have moved far away from home.

When my husband and I lived in the great northwest corner of the county and our families remained on the east coast, we began to include these invisible seniors in our holiday celebrations. Set an extra place at the dinner table for seniors living alone, fix a meal for them, visit and telephone on a regular basis, take them shopping, or drop them a card at birthday or holiday times. A few years ago, our church organized a seniors' ministry, initially to help our seniors take care of monthly necessities such as doctors' visits, banking, and market needs. It rapidly grew into weekly spiritual and social events, and now our seniors travel around the city to events such as crab feasts and ballroom dancing, and out of town to outlet shops, plays, and musicals. These seniors now operate our monthly food co-op, serving approximately ninety families, and a weekly food pantry ministry that serves five thousand hungry people annually. Reach out and people will reach back. There are some people you can shout an invitation to: "Y'all come on!" Others respond better to a note, a flyer, or a mailed personal written invitation; anonymous women tend to need personal one-on-one encouragement to separate them from living in the background.

When the Samaritan woman learned that Jesus was the long-awaited Messiah, she ran back to her village to tell everyone; she wanted them to know and to be included, but first she needed to reconnect with her community. As we come to the well in this generation, remember to stay connected and help others do the same. Susan had tried all sorts of things to solve her family problems; then she sat down on her front steps watching the neighborhood boys being coached by an older man, and it was as if God was speaking to her through the coach in the street. Susan had her answer and knew what she had to do. It was an ordinary moment with extraordinary consequences.

The Samaritan woman came to the well on an ordinary day, and there she met Jesus. Like Jesus, we need to make the necessary trips to find our sisters and brothers who have been forced from our midst, from our towns, and from our lives. We need to locate all the shut-offs and cut-offs, the HIV positives, AIDS victims, lonely seniors, abandoned children, overlooked supporters, body-smelling and glue-sniffing drug addicts, street walkers, and closet alcohol abusers. They are the invisible people we live around every day, but fail to notice. Take them to the well with you on your next trip to meet Jesus. Jesus intentionally went to Jacob's well to encounter the Samaritan woman, and just like Jesus we must intentionally reach out to the anonymous, wallpaper, background people among us.

CALL TO ACTION

The complexities of the daily dilemmas we face often drive us to the fringes of life. We would rather walk all over desolate terrain in the hot sun, allowing our problems to push us further and further from community, even from the Christ who waits for us at our wells of necessity. In our isolation we begin to believe that we are the only ones with our complex set of circumstances. Have you ever done that? We say things like "No one has it like me. I'm the only one struggling with this. Normal people don't go through these things. What have I done to deserve this? Why me and not them?" It's the isolation that teaches us to sing, "Nobody knows the trouble I've seen."

Well women: No matter how bad things get, don't cut yourself off from those around you. It is conceivable that the Samaritan woman closed and locked all the doors herself because of her lifestyle. Many of the women in the Circle of Love had lost their connections. They had no family, friends, or community to talk to, share with, or open up to. The other women in the Circle of Love provided them with a safe, caring community where they could blossom, something some of the women had never experienced before. They were not unlike the woman at the well. This sister-girlfriend had worn out her welcome in five different relationships. She failed to keep the lines of communication open with family, community, worship center, and God. She had burned all her bridges and she was down to her last man and her last hope. This woman was cut off, an island unto herself with only one way to get what she needed, rejecting conventional wisdom and walking away from her problems at strange hours, endangering herself in the heat of the day. Jesus will meet you when you least expect him at your well. Well women, even if you're down to your last bit of anything, hold on. Celebrate— you're becoming a woman of unexpected opportunity.

Discipline of the Well

Well Lesson

The first lesson of the well is that when you are a woman of unexpected opportunity it means being open to meeting the Divine anywhere, anytime. Even in desperate times God will wrap loving arms around us, calming the tumult and holding us close. When it seems God isn't there we may be looking too hard. Remember that it was in an ordinary moment—getting water—that Jesus met the Samaritan woman. God is in the everyday things. Listen, and be open to receiving God.

The second Well Lesson for well women is that learning to reach beyond what separates us from community and taking action to connect can change history. A shared experience will help you connect with others. Take small steps at first: Call someone before they even think to call you, invite someone out to eat rather than wait for an invitation, bring others into your personal space to share a book, video, CD, poem; go on a walk in the park, on the beach, or around the track at the high school. Become a part of a healing community, a church, or a small Christian fellowship, for it's in the healing community where you hear the testimony of those who have already ". . . walk[ed] through the valley of the shadow of death" (Psalm 23:4). It's in the healing community you realize that you are not the only one struggling with last things and it is in this community that reentry will be made easier. When you are ready, share your one hope with someone you trust, maybe a woman friend in your peer group, or an older woman who has already been "through many dangers, toils and snares." You just may find out that you are not the only one carrying an empty pitcher and one hope. Learn to reclaim the women in your community living anonymous lives. They are like the Samaritan woman; they are living invisible lives because of environment, illness, habits, seemingly overwhelming responsibilities, or catastrophes.

Well Words

Do not conform any longer to the pattern of this world, but be transformed by the renewing of your mind. Then you will be able to test and approve what God's will is—his good, and pleasing and perfect will.

ROMANS 12:2

And without faith it is impossible to please God, because anyone who comes to him must believe that he exists and that he rewards those who earnestly seek him.

HEBREWS 11:6

Your attitude should be the same as that of Christ Jesus.

PHILIPPIANS 2:5

Let the wicked forsake his way and the evil man his thoughts. Let him turn to the Lord, and he will have mercy on him, and to our God, for he will freely pardon. "For my thoughts are not your thoughts, neither are your ways my ways," declares the Lord.

ISAIAH 55:7–8

So you must also be ready . . .

MATTHEW 24:44

I stand at the door and knock. If anyone hears my voice and opens the door, I will come in.

REVELATION 3:20

. . . as we have the opportunity, let us do good . . .

GALATIANS 6:10

. . . make the most of every opportunity.

COLOSSIANS 4:5

Well Sabbatical

⟶ *Locate a quiet place and get into a comfortable position. Read Philippians 2:5 "Your attitude should be the same as that of Christ," or Isaiah 55:7–8, which reminds us that our thoughts are not like God's. You can also read 1 Kings 17 where Isaiah enters with the still small voice of God. Silence is precious. Be still in the silence. Listen for the God without, and the God within. The divine is present in every moment and in every place. God rewards those who earnestly seek Him (Hebrews 11:6).*

⟶ *Being calm with a chaotic mind is difficult. A disciplined mind begins when you seek to put into it what pleases God. Pray that God will grant you the mind of Christ when you face issues and make decisions. Seeking the mind of Christ requires surrendering to God's will. God's will is contained in God's Word and God will not ask you to do anything inconsistent with the nature and character of the Divine. God's desire is always for our highest good. Be still and release the controls of your life to the Transformer whose mercy endures forever; imagine yourself surrounded by loving, strong arms; relax in the embrace and gently lay your head upon the back of the chair as if you were laying your head upon your mother's breast. Be still and take deep breaths. When we are under stress we often forget to breathe deeply; hear the air expand your chest and rush through your*

nostrils. Be still and welcome the calm as you become one
with the universe.

Well Language

⌐ *God will meet me in my ordinary.*
⌐ *Anonymous is an unacceptable reality.*
⌐ *I am a woman open to God.*
⌐ *Reach out and people will reach back.*
⌐ *I am a woman looking for unexpected opportunity to ad-
vance!*

Well Work

1. *Take a meditation break daily. Be still for a change. Shield your
   eyes from the hot sun. Smell the air whip past you. Feel the sand
   as it falls over your sandaled feet. Look for the presence of God
   in your ordinary necessities. Be still, and listen to the still small
   voice of God.*
2. *Find three poems written by Anonymous; acknowledge and
   celebrate the authors in your own way.*
3. *Identify a woman in your community whose life, achievements,
   and contributions go unnoticed. Write her a thank you note for
   all her good works.*
4. *Speak to a woman who exists on the fringes of the community.
   Invite her into your world.*
5. *Instead of going to your regular lunch place, restaurant, market, library, movie theater, or video store go across town or into
   another neighborhood where you know no one and no one
   knows you. How do you feel?*
6. *Have you ever felt like an anonymous woman? Write in your*

journal about the seasons in your life when you wanted to disappear and disconnect from the community . . . and did!

7. Have you ever had an experience when you chose to decorate a situation or relationship like wallpaper covers a wall rather than take center stage? Write about it in your journal.

3

A Woman in Time

It was about the sixth hour.

JOHN 4:6

When our son Jon was four years old, my first cousin planned a big and beautiful wedding on the Eastern Shore of Maryland, which is known as the land of pleasant living. Jon was asked to be the ring bearer because, as the bride remarked, "He's old enough." He was fitted for his color-coordinated tuxedo, his shoes were polished, and his hair was cut. Jon rehearsed his part diligently, marching up and down the aisle of the church, clutching the little white satin pillow, finding his place at the altar, standing straight with the best man's hand resting on his shoulder. On the morning of the wedding, Jon was ready to go. The musicians began playing the wedding march, and my husband led Jon to his place at the top of the aisle. All heads turned and eyes were focused upon the chocolate cherub holding the satin pillow with two wedding bands securely pinned to it. The congregation looked at Jon and Jon looked back. And Jon refused to move. No amount of coaxing could get him to walk down the aisle and finally the satin pillow was given to the flower girls, who played both parts very well. A year later, Jon was asked again to serve as ring bearer for his kindergarten teacher. With the last wedding stage fright still on our minds, we tried to discourage her, but

61

she would not accept no for an answer, and sure enough Jon was fitted for his tuxedo.

Sometimes it's hard to know when is the right time. The Samaritan woman should have been going to the well in the early morning hours when it was cool outside, but for a variety of reasons she decided noon was the time to get water at the well. Noon was the hottest part of the day; it was the wrong hour. In this chapter you will meet the Divine waiting for you at your well of necessity as we look into God's timing, who's in control of our destiny, developing a well consciousness, and being aware of our kairos moments.

Your kairos is waiting for you.

WRONG HOUR, RIGHT TIME

The Samaritan woman was oblivious to what time it was in her life. It looked like it was the wrong time of day from the hot noon sun, but it was the right time for Divine intervention. The other women inside of her, the one-hope woman, the last-things woman, the anonymous woman, and the unexpected-opportunity woman, the open-to-God woman were having a theophany, a personal confrontation with the Divine. It was her time; it was time to seize the moment; it was the right time in her life according to God, and more women were about to be added to her collage.

Charlene had a beautiful calendar with full double pages for each day of the week, laminated tabs for each month, and color-coded highlights. She diligently filled in the minutes, hours, and days on her schedule as meetings, events, family obligations, responsibilities, church duties, and holidays came and went. The months passed quickly and she felt ready for each full day as it approached. Yet Charlene sensed that something was missing; she checked her calendar but couldn't see anything that she had forgotten to do. Had she forgotten to write something down? Was there an opportunity she had passed by without noticing? She couldn't quite put her finger on it. Was it the wrong hour, right time?

Charlene had every waking hour timed to perfection. Her life ran according to the clock. She was never too early, too late, but always on time. Every detail was planned and timed by clock and calendar. She sensed that she was living either one step ahead or behind everything. Her clock got her to the right meeting on time but she came with the wrong materials or ideas others were not ready to receive. The calendar guided her to the right activity but she had a nagging feeling that she should be doing other things.

Charlene was channel surfing her life. She was so hurried that she was clicking from one event to the next, never staying long enough to look beyond the surface to sense the move of God in her life. She was so caught up in the superficial that she missed the spiritual. She was getting things done but never benefited from the experiences.

Click! She was up and out of bed and up and out of the house without breakfast, prayer, or greetings to others. *Click!* She eats breakfast at her desk while she shuffles papers, returns telephone calls, answers her e-mails, and delegates busy work to other staff members. *Click!* She goes to her staff meeting on time. *Click!* She updates her Palm-Pilot during the presentation. *Click!* The meeting is over and while others go to lunch together, she eats lunch getting her hair and nails done. *Click!* She takes work home, does the wash, dyes her hair, and makes out an extensive to do list before going to bed. *Click!* She wants to change but if she could she would have done it a long time ago. *Click!* She didn't know how.

Well women are women in time, not merely on time. When it's the right time opportunities previously denied reoccur; résumés are reviewed, positions offered, second chances extended, and new ideas seem to materialize out of thin air. When it is the right time, people you need to see become available, doors that were shut open, productivity rises, and possibilities abound. When it is the right time, chance meetings become life-changing encounters. Life runs more smoothly when you find yourself at the right place, and in the right place at the right time. Problems seem solvable; burdens are lighter; and the future brighter. When you are out of time, time crawls, you complain about every little thing and grumble about every change, your efforts are halfhearted, your completion rate drops, work goes more slowly, mistakes increase because your concentration is on vacation, and you tend to give lip service instead of sincere service. Whenever you are out of time, it's best just to tread water. The time may not be right, and you may not be ready; people or resources may not be in the right position. It is best to wait, learning during the lull, until it is God's time. Remember, the current that took you out into deep waters can also bring you back to shore again.

WHO CONTROLS OUR DESTINY?

Here we find a woman walking in the heat of the day with the one hope that one day things would change. If she could have changed things on her own she would have, and if others could have changed it for her, they would have. She couldn't move forward; she couldn't retreat; she lived at the mercy of past decisions and at the behest of others, and all she could do was show up at an ungodly hour at Jacob's well. Jacob had dug this well out of solid rock centuries before Jesus stopped by for a rest and some water. This deep cylinderlike hole reached beyond the surface barrenness to saturated regions that yielded water, water that was necessary to live. There were no limousines, taxis, subways, or automobiles to assist in traveling great distances. Jesus and the disciples, Peter, Philip, Nathaniel, and Andrew, walked in the heat of the day. Clouds of dust rose from the movement of sandaled feet over the well-worn paths and created halos of haze around them as they pushed their way north. The desert can be a monotonous menu of heat, dust, wind, beige, brown, and thirst, a rugged terrain only adding to the burden already at hand. Jesus, who is God and now man, was very tired and weary from the journey as he stopped his entourage at the well. Imagine him leaning against the well, seeking the cool of the rocks or shade from a nearby shadow, the extreme heat producing the sensation of dryness in his mouth and throat. Creation sits and the universe pauses as one hope comes to the well.

The Samaritan woman needed a liberator to free her from the bondage of her culture and lifestyle; her destiny, her meeting with Jesus gave her freedom. She was not the first generation of people to be liberated by God. Years before when Moses went from his home in pharaoh's house to Goshen, he acted at the wrong time. Moses tried to force his leadership upon the Hebrews in Goshen during their season of slavery in Egypt, but it was not his time. Forty years later, he returned from the Midian desert as a liberator. It was no longer his idea, but God's idea, and this time he was commissioned and empowered by God.

Today we sometimes think life is easier than it was hundreds of years ago. And in many ways it is. But has our destiny really changed? Biblical times were characterized by gathering wood to provide heat, heating stones to bake bread, using oil lamps for light, and drawing water to drink from a well. Nowadays, we have the flexibility of lighting the night thanks to electricity, lightbulbs, and other modern inventions. We can work in full light the whole night long if we choose to, using modern machinery like personal computers, fax machines, front end loaders, laser surgery, self-cleaning ovens, and microwaves to ease our labor. Still we work hard, must sleep, and need a Redeemer. In ancient times life was much different than it is today; and then again, people were very much the same. People worked hard, needed sleep, and they needed a Redeemer. We still need a Redeemer if we are to find our ultimate destiny. "You see, at just the right time, when we were still powerless, Christ died for the ungodly" (Romans 5:6). At just the right time, Jesus was at the well for this woman from Samaria.

Charlene and the Samaritan woman lived at different times. One lived in ancient times and the other contemporary. The former was living and working by the clock and calendar. She lived according to *her* time. The other had unwittingly stepped into God's perfect timing at the well. "For in due season we will reap if we faint now" (Galatians 6:9).

Was it destiny? Was it fate? Was it a coincidence or a Divine appointment set eons ago by God? It was all Divine! It does not matter whether one lives in ancient times or in the twenty-first century; whenever it is God's time, it's time!

* * *

The Samaritan woman went somewhere without going anywhere and the going changed her life forever. She was on a simple journey, an ordinary trip to accomplish a necessary thing—fetching a pail of water. The Samaritan woman hoped for change, but could not change on her own because personal transformation requires the intervention of the Divine. She met Jesus, the Son of the living God, who took the necessary risks to meet her at Jacob's well. Whenever God intervenes in the lives of creation, an ordinary situation changes into an extraordinary encounter.

KAIROS MOMENTS

Kairos (kī-räs) is a Greek word that refers to the appointed time; it is the right time, the fullness of time, the time of opportunity for action or exchange, unrestricted by the passing of time. In chronological time, a person is legally an adult by the age of twenty-one. Authentic adult maturity may arrive at a kairos time of twenty-five, thirty, forty-two, or fifty-five years of age. Chronology is concrete. Kairos is abstract. Many of us are unconscious of those times in our lives when it is "our time." We get so caught up in the chronology of our necessities that we don't discern the kairos moments. "You know how to interpret the appearance of the sky, but you cannot interpret the signs of the times," said Jesus (Matthew 16:3). Chronology is the linear continuity of time; it is the inevitable succession of moments, minutes, hours, days, weeks, months, and years; it is the flow of seasons and history.

Chronology is a human attempt to systematize the order of God's creation. God, who existed before time, created time. The Creator made two entities: day and night. The sun ruled the day and the moon presided over the night. The Bible is silent on the length of each entity.

Chronology is mankind's attempt to measure time in an orderly fashion within God's creation using external resources. Chronology is a valuable tool in the hands of human beings. Chronology is determined by flesh. Kairos is time determined by the Eternal.

The due dates for the births of each of my three children were inconsequential. They were merely ETAs, estimated times of arrival. Each child arrived either before or long after their due date. It was always attributed to miscounting the days of the last menses.

I believe each child arrived at a kairos moment, a time God determined. At just the right moment each child made an entrance into this world, not by accident or miscalculation but by the kairos arrangement of God.

We tend to be unconscious of our kairos moments, having no idea when our time arrives, or our time to change begins. We are unaware of our time to be blessed, our time of ovulation, or when we are most receptive to being pregnant with new ideas, chances, and changes. Charlene was so busy changing channels that she was unaware of kairos moments. The tragedy of being ignorant of our kairos is that when it's over, it's over. The window of destiny will close, the weather change, the world turn, and the universe wax and wane. The river will never be in the same place twice. The kairos moment may never return again; we need to develop our sensitivity to our kairos moments. We should be sensitive to when we will receive the seed of God's possibilities into the uterus of our minds, our time to bud and to blossom, our time to bear fruit and harvest, our time to lie fallow, and our time to till the field and make ready for the planting of a new crop.

There is the kairos of spring: a season of new beginnings. The kairos of summer: the season of ripening. The kairos of autumn: the season of productivity. The kairos of winter: the season of renewal. There may be no external indications of the kairos of opportunity and decision, no change in the environment or relationships, no visible signs, warning bells, whistles, or alarms, but you can discern the time by being in relationship with the Timekeeper.

It is through your relationship with God that you become attuned to the changes in spiritual time and temperature. Our kairos moments are in the hands of the Divine, the orchestrator of time (Psalm 31:15). God, who is the creator of chronology, existed before recorded time and will continue long after time ceases. God is the master of Eternity. In the fullness of time, he sent his son Jesus through Samaria to meet this woman at Jacob's well. God is the determiner, deciding the moment, people, and places to advance his purpose. God is the one who determines the kairos. There is a time for everything; a time to be born and a time to die; a time to begin and a time to end; a time to let go and a time to hold on; a time to start again and a time to quit; and a time to fight back and a time to defend (Ecclesiastes 3:1–11).

The Samaritan woman came to the well at the wrong time of day, but it was the right time in her life for change. She may have been living on the wrong side of five failed relationships and one current shady one, but it was the right time for transformation. Jesus chose this woman, at this time and place, to guide her through the process of personal transformation. It begins at the appointed hour, the kairos moment. It was a kairos moment for the Samaritan woman; it was her time. It was the wrong hour to come to the well, but it was the right time. Because the Jewish day ran from six in the morning until six in the evening, the sixth hour would make it twelve o'clock, high noon. The human body is under the most physical stress at this time of the day from dehydration, heat, and the blinding sun all working together to create discomfort. Her inability to flow in the socioeconomic exchange of her society rendered her anonymous—a nameless, faceless, hopeless woman, trying to avoid the stares, gossips, and whispers of her community. It was the wrong hour and she was the wrong woman with the wrong lifestyle, but it was her time. The disciples were gone and no other travelers were on the road, no passing caravans were around, no wandering strangers or community residents could be seen, just Jesus and her. It was her kairos moment.

When our son Jon was asked again to be ring bearer, this time for his kindergarten teacher, he rehearsed his part diligently and took his place at the head of the wedding party. The music started, the people stared, and this time, he walked down the aisle, a perfect gentleman. He stole the hearts of everyone and practically stole the show from the bride. The first time, he had been old enough, but he hadn't been ready; the second time was a kairos moment—it was his time and he *was* ready. Life can be a blur if you live only by the clock and the calendar. Remember, live life as a marathon, not a sprint. Be spiritually attentive to God's times and seasons in your life.

Laura kept her eyes and her heart open to the presence of God. Curling her hair, drinking coffee, watching the sun set, walking through a dirty alley, passing a beggar on the street, nursing her baby, teaching her child to tie a shoe, daydreaming on a summer afternoon, or sitting on the front porch on a summer's evening; she expected God to show up, unexpected. It might have been the wrong hour, but when God spoke it was the right time! A Scripture would drop into her spirit, a thought would come with other thoughts quickly flooding her mind, like too much melted snow forcing a river to expand beyond its boundaries at springtime. She was open and listening for the still small voice of God to speak in her life. She was aware of her kairos. She was becoming a woman open to God.

A woman in time is not driven by the human organization of time. She is cognizant of its usefulness and constraints but she has learned that when it's God's time, things flow easier; a flower blooms, visions are realized, and plans come together. When she does it on her own time, she may get things done but it will be the hard way. A woman in time has learned to live by the promptings of the Holy Spirit to let her know when to turn aside to see what God is doing. It is like Moses, who was busy tending cattle on the back side of a mountain in the Median desert. He was not too busy to notice a burning bush and turn aside. When he did, he got a new assignment as the chief executive of Let My People Go Inc., headquartered back in Egypt. Moses was able to look beyond the daily routine to see God's wonder. When the Samaritan saw Jesus at the well, she did not retreat or busy herself with water hauling but kept walking toward her destiny because it was her time.

CALL TO ACTION

Don't miss the Divine waiting for you at your well of necessity. It may appear like an ordinary day, feel like just another trip to the store, or sound like just another task to complete. On the surface it's just another bus, train, or subway ride somewhere, but listen with spiritual ears and look with spiritual eyes beyond the sand, sun, and constant well necessities in your life. The next time you are at a place, scratch beneath the surface of a visitation; ask God to show you what you have been missing. When you are on your way somewhere, ask God to make you acutely conscious of missed chances for relationships or encounters with the spiritual in the midst of the sacred. The time and place may be providing an unexpected opportunity to experience something new. The Samaritan woman came to the well at the wrong time of day, but it was the right time in her life for change. The Divine was waiting for her, just as God waits for each of us at our well of necessity. It may appear like an ordinary day, but listen with spiritual ears and look with spiritual eyes beyond the constant well necessities in your life.

My grandmother had two claims to fame in the kitchen: her great applesauce and her home-baked bread. When she baked bread she'd mix yeast into the dough and set it aside. As time passed, the dough would rise and be ready for the oven. If the dough went into the oven before rising, it would not become what it was created to be—bread. The yeast needed time to work unseen within the dough, changing its character and consistency. You do not see the yeast but if you give it time, you will see the results.

Our life is the dough in the hands of our Savior. Jesus kneads us into new creatures and the Holy Spirit is the yeast working on the inside to change our character.

Yeast needs time to ready the dough to take the heat. The heat of the oven could cause the dough to fall flat but because it goes into the oven when it is time, it rises *with* the heat instead of falling. Jesus needs time to prepare us to transform what could destroy us into something that helps us become what the Lord created us to be. You do not see the Spirit working on the inside, but give Him time and you will see the results.

At the kairos moment we do not fall but rise in the heat of the battle. God determines the moment of readiness, never too soon and never too late.

Our kairos moments are in the hands of God, the one who determines a time for everything. Develop a well consciousness, and be aware of kairos occasions. Become a woman open to God.

Discipline of the Well

Well Lesson

The first lesson from the well is being a woman in time, not just on time. Develop a well consciousness, looking beyond the present reality to the unseen hand of God moving behind the scenes of your life. Be open and conscious of the present moment, seeking God in that moment by asking the Master of Eternity how you can take advantage of what lies before you. Evaluate where you are. Look to see what time it is in your life.

Our second lesson from the well is to be aware of kairos occasions. Is this the kairos moment to retreat, retrench, or move full steam ahead? You can pay attention to God's prompting or you can remain oblivious to life as it happens every day. It was the Samaritan woman's time. It was time to seize the moment, and it was the right time in her life according to God. Listen to what God says to you this week.

Well Words

Teach us to number our days aright that we may gain a heart of wisdom.

PSALM 90:12

Be very careful, then, how you live—not as unwise but as wise, making the most of every opportunity, because the days are evil.

EPHESIANS 5:15-16

But when the time had fully come, God sent his Son, born of a woman, born under law, . . .

GALATIANS 4:4

Let us not become weary in doing good, for at the proper time we will reap a harvest if we do not give up.

GALATIANS 6:9

All of the days of my hard service, I will wait for my renewal to come.

JOB 14:14

Wait for the Lord; be strong and take heart and wait for the Lord.

PSALM 27:14

Well Sabbatical

⁓ Take your sabbatical outside if you can. Sit and listen to the silence in a secure place. Smell the silence, hear the silence, and record your thoughts in your travel log. Always remember that you can take your sabbatical on the road. Whenever you come across a space that seems inviting take a rest and enjoy it.

Well Language

Write these affirmations on five-by-seven file cards with a felt-tip pen in a color you absolutely adore. Place them strategically at home or work. They can be your private affirmations or you may want to share them with others as an encouraging act of kindness.

> ⌒ *In God's time, my change will come.*
> ⌒ *My times are in the hands of God.*
> ⌒ *I will not run ahead of God, but will run with God.*
> ⌒ *What time is it?*
> ⌒ *Don't let this moment pass me by.*
> ⌒ *Hold on, change is coming!*

Well Work

1. *Rituals are older than any language. They are patterned movements that reflect what you believe. "The Lord said to Moses, 'Speak to Aaron and say to him, "When you set up the seven lamps, they are to light the area in front of the lampstand"'" (Numbers 8:1–2).*

   We believe that Jesus is the light of the world. We also believe His command to let our light so shine that others may see our good works and Glorify our God in heaven (Matthew 5:16).

   Tonight, when the house is quiet, play your favorite sacred CD or tape. Light a candle so that the light is thrown forward to remind yourself that women open to God remember to face forward. Tomorrow let the light of Jesus shine through you and take no credit for what God does in or through you.

2. *Read one passage of scripture from Well Words. Enjoy a quiet meditative moment focused upon that scripture.*

3. *Ask God, What time is it in your life? Pray that you will become aware of your kairos moments so opportunities won't pass you by. Take advantage of every kairos moment.*

4. *Record on one side of a five-by-seven file card a moment when you thought you were old enough or ready for something, and it didn't happen. Things were not falling into place and you may have become bitter, edgy, or upset by the stall. On the other side, write down when it was your time, when things fell into place because it was your season, your time. Record more of your kairos moments.*

5. *Place the cards on your collage along with any objects that represent your kairos occasions. For example, dried flowers from a special moment, ticket stubs, photographs, your baby's sock, a wedding invitation, the résumé that led to the career you're trained for or wanted, leaves from the tree outside your new home or apartment.*

6. *Write in your journal about your kairos moments.*

4

A Woman Pregnant with the Possibilities of God

~~~

When a Samaritan woman came to draw water, Jesus said to her . . .

JOHN 4:7

As a young girl growing up in Baltimore, I lived near the heart of the African American community. Our neighborhood was filled with beautiful homes with marble steps that had to be washed weekly, and it was these same steps that we were to climb promptly at twilight. You remember the days when you were put to bed while it was still light outside in the summertime? I grew up in a neighborhood with mostly boys and only one other girl my best friend, Irma. I learned at a very young age that the name of the game was survival—survival of the fittest. In our neighborhood, survival of the fittest meant being able to do the things the boys were doing, and to do them well. We ran, climbed, jumped, played ball, and rode bicycles like bats out of hell.

At a certain age—somewhere around puberty—we were taught that young ladies didn't play games with the boys, but sat, watched, and applauded them. We learned that even if we knew something, we should fake ignorance so the boys could shine. We learned that we should not answer all the questions in class if we wanted dates to the prom. We learned that if we were smart it was better not to appear smart—we'd get more flies with honey than with brain matter. The lesson we received was to live our lives through the boys, to please the boys, and not to follow the instructions of God or our ambitions to satisfy ourselves.

The Samaritan woman might have preferred to have a surrogate go to the well for her because she knew people would gossip about her or that she might run into others who looked down on her. But God had other plans for her. He broke her out of her life of fear, a life that had led to surrogate living, and in one moment she became her own birth mother by living for Jesus, not for others. She carried her own weight by fulfilling her potential and meeting Jesus at the well.

Are you fulfilling your potential? Do you need to stop trying to make up for something or fix or change your past and identify what's missing from your life today? This chapter will encourage you to become pregnant with God's possibilities, stop surrogating your life away, and start to carry the weight; you can be your own birth mother. The Samaritan woman did it. You can do it too!

SURROGATE LIVING

Colleen did not plan on losing sight of her dreams, but they seemed to be fading away anyway. She had promised her father she would finish college after she got married at nineteen, but slowly and without realizing it, she replaced her own dreams with the needs of her growing family. When her sons were grown with families and lives of their own, Colleen was faced with rediscovering herself, her marriage, and her dreams. It wasn't a well experience, but getting that diploma allowed her to come to terms with herself as she came to a new stage and age.

Emily just decided one day not to participate in her life any more; she had no energy left to confront life's battles, so she stayed away from church, family, neighbors, and friends, doing a better job escaping than Houdini. She quit her book club, shopped at the twenty-four-hour grocery store at midnight, came and left work as unobtrusively as she could, and didn't answer or return phone calls. She taped soap operas during the day and spent her evenings and weekends watching them. She lived her life via the soaps. She was impossible to find.

Have you ever allowed other people or things to run your life? Some women let their husbands or mothers make all the choices for them, and they lose control of their own lives. Some women try to live through their children. Or the children become their excuse not to do more to fulfill their potential.

Ami was way out of control doing whatever needed to happen so her kids could sport one-hundred-dollar Air Jordans. She gave up vacation to send the kids to camp, while taking part-time work to supplement her regular job so they could be raised in the style she thought they deserved. One day, when they were grown and gone, she had no one to clothe, feed, clean, or sacrifice and suffer for. There is something to be said for living your own life.

Submerging your life into a surrogate, such as your spouse, may do wonders for your spouse's ego temporarily, but one day you'll wake up and smell the cappuccino. Bob basically carried life for Helen, the seed and the deed. Bob made the money, paid the bills, went to school to get that promotion. When it came to Helen there wasn't much to say. Bob's career was more important than hers, so she gave up career opportunities and promotions to join the right clubs, make friends with the right people, score brownie points with his superiors, and chair the right committee in the community. No one in this relationship had ever discussed compromise.

Surrogate living is giving your life over to someone else. It's what the Samaritan woman did because she didn't know how to move beyond her circumstances. Surrogate living means you rest your destiny upon a surrogate's ability to carry your life to full term, and you submit your future to the womb of another human being's risks and fortunes. Sometimes a surrogate wants to keep the finished product since the surrogate did the work, endured the labor, and now wants the reward. Imagine the custody battle of figuring out whose life it is anyway! The surrogate carried you for days, weeks, months, years; the surrogate wiped your tears, held your hand, mentored, coached, suggested, demanded, cloned, gave you a terrific makeover—you were such a great Eliza Doolittle. The surrogate did what you were afraid to do or couldn't do yourself, and now your life is not your life anymore; your life is the surrogate's life; now you must return the investment by living it on the surrogate's terms. Surrogate living is appealing to women who have lost the energy to confront life, like Emily deciding not to participate in her own life anymore. The keys of our queendom are surrendered to boyfriends, parents, spouses, children, relatives, and other men and women who drift in and out of our lives. Power is given to them to organize and orchestrate everything from the minute to the meaningful. While Bob was working on his life, he developed skills and stamina, gifts and interests, and gained strength to meet the challenges in his life and Helen's life. Helen, on the other hand, remained weak.

Women surrender to surrogates because they are afraid to live their own lives. They are unwilling or unable to carry their own pots to the well. If you always wanted to _____ (fill in the blank), but instead you train, nurture, and guide your children to be what you dreamed of being, then they are your surrogates carrying the life that you did not carry for yourself. Surrogate living is living your life through their lives. They have a life playing football, entering beauty pageants, taking voice lessons, going to law school, becoming doctors, but what do you have?

The Samaritan woman found herself avoiding people at the well because of her reputation. Submitting to unhealthy relationships because it feels better than being alone is not the way to live. You move into his place because it's free and he provides space and companionship, since you're unable to carry life alone. You're not even trying to audition to be his wife, but something is better than nothing. Everyone makes choices for you because you believe you are not worthy or good enough to make your own choices. You avoid confronting life issues because of poor decisions made in the past, and you've tried doing it on your own, but it just did not work out. The divorce became final, the baby died, he's married and not about to leave his wife and just forgot to tell you, the office romance didn't work out the way you thought it would and now everyone thinks you were trying to sleep your way to the top. The low life has a high price tag; get a life of your own.

Some women spend their whole lives hoping to send someone else to live in their place, let someone else go to the interview, write the report, raise the kids, rub his back, and rotate his tires. They live in the wonderful land of if onlys: if only I had enough money I would do this, if only I had a husband I wouldn't have to do that, if only I hadn't had children so soon, if only I had a degree, if only I had a house, if only I had another job, if only I had someone to handle this for me, if only I had the support I really needed. If only I had a better career, a promotion, a raise, loyal friends, I wouldn't have to spend so much time struggling to get the necessities at the alternative wells of life. I know women who have opted for surrogate living because they believe they need a man in their lives to come home to, look up to, share with, cut the grass, put oil in the car, and to have and to hold from this day forth. They believe a woman is just not complete unless she has a man, and so they put their lives on hold. These women live to see themselves reflected in a man's eyes. The problem is that too often it's just any man, someone else's man, or one already taken by drugs, violence, prison, or laziness. Somewhere along the line we have been taught that smart is ugly, and high achievement has translated into the low social life. Women will put their lives on hold or surrogate them out until The Man comes along. They don't buy their own homes, stocks, or land. They don't pursue a degree because they are waiting for The Man and are afraid they won't be attractive as a business owner with a professional degree because if they can do these things, there will be nothing else for The Man to do. How can you be adding to your collage when your life is on hold? Colleen did not plan on losing sight of her dream to get a college degree, but without a plan to get it done her dream was almost lost.

If you find yourself in life's quagmire, the Bible gives Good News that will help you out. It affirms that in Christ Jesus, you are complete. You have been given fullness in Christ (Colossians 2:10). Luke's Gospel proclaims that God sent the angel Gabriel to a virgin named Mary, who was betrothed to Joseph, a member of the House of David. In the Christian tradition, it is believed that the angel told Mary she would conceive and bear a son who would be called Jesus, the Son of the Most High. Mary could hardly believe that she could get pregnant without having sexual relations, and in the Judaic tradition, a woman betrothed must be sexually pure or she could be publicly stoned to death. It was inconceivable that a virgin would risk her life, reputation, and future to engage in the passions of the flesh. " 'How will this be,' Mary asked the angel, 'since I am a virgin.' The angel answered, 'The Holy Spirit will come upon you, and the power of the Most High will overshadow you. So the holy one to be born will be called the Son of God' " (Luke 1:34–35). This is called the Immaculate Conception, the miraculous birth of the Messiah, Jesus the Christ. This birth defied physiological and biological realities. The debate about the Immaculate Conception will probably rage on; however, it is the opinion of many scholars, including Dr. Cain Hope Felder and William Barclay, that the Holy Spirit impregnated Mary without a man's participation. If the Holy Spirit can bring new life through Mary without the participation of Joseph, certainly he can give you an abundant life without the presence or participation of a sperm donor. Still many women fail to live life fully, but remain waiting for male participation.

The lesson we girls received in our old Baltimore neighborhood to live our lives through the boys, to please the boys, and not to follow our God or our ambitions to satisfy ourselves totally misses the point of life. Male companionship, male friends, boyfriends, and husbands are one of God's best ideas, but until a healthy, loving relationship that promotes your full potential happens, resist the urge to become a perpetual lady in waiting, never living fully, and never feeling complete or whole. Live your life to the fullest—now and always.

BE YOUR OWN BIRTH MOTHER

Several years ago my father and mother died, a year apart. My father died first, and twelve months later my mother died. Mother's sudden death was particularly hard to take, as she had been my best friend and confidante. She was the one who played back my sermons to me when my shield of faith was lowered, or, when I forgot what God's Word said, she was diligent in repeating it back to me. As Romans 10:17 says, "Consequently, faith comes from hearing the message, and the message is heard through the word of Christ." But now the one who knew me best no longer lived in this life. The one who could tell me how I was doing or what was happening in my life by the sound of my voice or the look in my eye no longer walked this Earth. My mother, the one who could appreciate who I had become because she knew me back in the day, was silenced on this side of glory.

I decided to become my own birth mother. The psalmist reminds us that when our mothers and fathers forsake us, God will take up the slack (Psalm 27). The thought of being my own birth mother took the edge off my feeling of abandonment. I could have sung "Sometimes I Feel Like a Motherless Child," but I'd rather sing "I'm Pregnant with the Possibilities of God." Now I am the womb of my own existence, fertile and ripe. I am one flesh with the man God joined to me in a covenant relationship and together we parent three children, but I am also birth mother of my own today and my own tomorrow.

Through receiving Living Water the Samaritan woman learned that she needed to be her own birth mother. Her failed marriages and current unsatisfying relationship were not the life for her. Jesus provided the love and acceptance she needed to cross the bridge of personal transformation. Through his friendship she began to see that she deserved a better life and better treatment that she had expected for herself.

Being your own birth mother requires that you give of yourself. It takes hard work, determination, nurturing, time, and patience—you are worth it! Be sure to give ample time for gestation as God's Word plants new ideas, possibilities, and power within you. There is time between the planting and the harvest, and between the pregnancy and the delivery. Give God's Word a resting place in your spirit by adjusting your daily routine to include time spent reading, studying, and reflecting on the Word of God. Be careful what you allow your eyes to see and ears to hear; dwell on whatever is pure, honest, lovely, true, just, and honorable (Philippians 4:8). Feed the seed of the Spirit rather than the need of the flesh.

Remember Colleen and her dream to finish college? She did it, but it wasn't easy. Being your own birth mother can be a lot of work. In Colleen's case, it took time, money, determination, focus, and a lot of self-love before she was able to walk across the stage, diploma in hand. Her smile said it all.

In the physical world, a birth mother must be careful about diet and other substances. A pregnant woman must be conscious of exercise and weight, and she must plan for adequate rest. She adjusts her daily routine to accommodate the baby's growth. So too must a spiritual birth mother adjust her daily routine in order to carry her life to full term and to its full potential. She may not realize it, but God is birthing in her possibilities she never imagined. She wants God to find her capable of growing into His vision for her life. Without a vision, a woman perishes, but with a vision, she prospers. Where there is no revelation, the people cast off restraint (Proverbs 29:18). You can be birth mother to the seeds of possibility the Holy Spirit plants in your womb all by yourself. The Holy Spirit can plant ideas, innovations, inventions, gifts, skills, talents, events, visions, dreams, and all kinds of things you have never thought or heard of before.

If you've had a child or gone through the experience with a friend, you know what it's like to be pregnant for the first time. The swollen ankles, nausea, tiredness, wacky hormones, and stretch marks are wearing. Giving birth is hard; it's hard on the body, the emotions, and the mind. With all there is to accomplish before the arrival of a baby it's a good thing God planned nine months' notice to get used to the idea.

The weight of growing life in the womb often leaves stretch marks like deflated spider veins across the stomach. The stretch marks of life are caused by the many challenges that add to our load in life. Stressors that come our way, both internal and external—like working overtime, receiving unexpected guests, returning phone calls, hives, pimples, sick kids, migraines, midlife crises, menopause, promotions, or business downsizing and pink slips—all challenge us on a daily basis. The stretch marks indicate that we were able to expand and operate with an extra load. This new capacity allows us to handle the rapid and persistent growth, change, and movement during this time. The marks show we were able to shift weight to achieve balance in our life, that we sacrificed space to make room for expanding responsibilities and consequences.

Birthing new ideas, new dreams, new visions, and new realities is possible only when you begin to love God and love yourself. Tap into God's creative spirit. Women who refuse to let their lives be defined by habit, history, or heritage and instead strive to become what God created them to be, find God's creative spirit at their fingertips to help them along the way. You can't love or be loved if you don't love yourself. Live your own life, learn to admire the stretch marks as signs of your ability to grow, and learn to nurture yourself with the help of Jesus.

CARRYING THE WEIGHT

Modern scientists are credited with developing the discipline of psychology and the studies of human nature, when really they have been uncovering what Jesus developed centuries before. Jesus fully understands the human psyche and continually fills our lives with kairos moments. The Samaritan woman reminds us that personal transformation takes place when individuals are willing to spend time with God. The

Divine stands behind his word. Living life through Jesus is a productive venture. It is about learning to live life empowered by the strength of God, not your own strength. In Christ, ". . . whoever loses his life for my sake will find it" (Matthew 10:39). The psalmist proclaims that we are fearfully and wonderfully made (Psalm 139). We are uniquely created in the image of God and our uniqueness is fashioned so that no two finger-prints are alike. The hairs upon our heads are numbered and it was in our mother's womb that God knew us.

Do not give life away, live it. You were created for a purpose that only you can fulfill. No one else can do what God has created you to do. You may try to pass it on to others, but God created you to be the exception, not the rule, in life. You were created to innovate, not merely dupli-cate what has already been done. To do this, you must be open to living life to its fullest, even if it means you must go to the well by yourself in the heat of the day because you can't afford to have a servant go in your place. Colleen got her college degree. It was satisfying to her, it gave her sons the example of a strong woman, and everyone was proud of her. Only you can occupy the space that God created for you: You and the Holy Spirit labor together with your promise of abundant life. In the full-ness of time, when The Man chosen for you from the foundations of the universe enters your life, you'll have more to bring to the table of your re-lationship as a woman, and not just a lady in waiting for life. You won't be handing him the collage of a life filled with photos produced by your surrogate. As your own birth mother, you'll have more and you'll be more. As little girls Irma and I didn't hesitate to jump into the neighbor-hood and live life to the fullest. It was different from what other girls were doing but we adapted to our environment. So why give up that survival-of-the-fittest attitude? Keep the spirit.

Mary placed herself in a position to be blessed with life. When God's angel announced to her the imminent pregnancy without partici-pation from a man, she responded, "I am the Lord's servant. May it be to me as you have said" (Luke 1:38). Mary was willing to receive the impossi-ble; she was open to the absurd because she had faith that God would stand behind his word. She risked her reputation and her impending marriage to Joseph to carry this life, and her receptivity paved the way for the reconciliation between Heaven and Earth.

As the heat rises from the desert floor and fills her mouth and nostrils with suffocating temperatures beneath her veil, the Samaritan woman's eyes focus on a stranger at her well and a wave of fear ripples across her countenance. She was so sure no one else was going to be at the fork in the road outside the city. If she were wealthy, she would have sent a servant to fetch the day's water, but the Samaritan woman did not have a servant to carry her pots to the well or to help her take care of her household responsibilities. She had to carry her own pots and haul her own water. She could not exempt herself from going to get water, just as we should not exempt ourselves from living our own lives. She changed wells from the one in the city to the one outside the city, but she still had to get water. It was an ordinary moment that precipitated a crisis. Her carefully constructed disappearing act was failing. Someone had broken through her mask of anonymity, and the exclusionary, historical, religious, and gender-dividing walls were coming down. As the Samaritan woman came to draw water, Jesus became the hidden opportunity to a new life and history, one where she would leave behind her previous ways. Jesus was there to trigger redemption, the hidden potential of transformation that lay just below the surface of her life, like the water that bubbled below the surface of Jacob's well.

CALL TO ACTION

The Bible, God's standard operating procedures manual, gives the standard operating procedures for life. The manual says that you are created in the image of God—reflect it (Genesis 9:6), you are fearfully and wonderfully made—act like it (Psalm 139:14), you are endowed with intelligence—so use it (Genesis 2:19), you were created for God's pleasure and glory—praise him (Revelation 4:11), you are made equal in Christ Jesus and are complete in him—trust it (Colossians 2:10), and you can have abundant life—make the most of it (John 10:10). You are a mist that appears for a little while and then vanishes (James 4:14). Where you spend eternity depends upon the faith decisions you make in this life. It is the Divine that grants life and every day above ground is a good day.

The seed planted by the Holy Spirit, watered by stretching toward right living, and nurtured by the belief and faith that God is able, reaps a harvest of rewards. The Divine stands behind the Word and will seek to perform it readily. God's Word has within it the ability, the energy, and the life force to effect creative works in your life. Psalm 55:22 reminds us that Jesus is our burden bearer. "Cast your cares on the Lord and he will sustain you; he will never let the righteous fall." God is able to do more than we can ask. Too many of us simply surrogate our lives to someone else rather than trust God to strengthen the muscles of our womb, so that we can bear the weight of life.

The Chinese word for crisis consists of two characters. One represents danger and the other represents hidden opportunity. They often seem to go together in life. You can turn off the telephone and go to bed depressed because of the twists and turns of life or you can stretch out on God's Word, which reminds us that weeping may endure for a night, but joy is expected in the morning (Psalm 30:5). Where you used to panic, you pray, and where you used to quote Jerry Springer or Montel Williams, you now quote the Bible. The Spirit of God still hovers over the void of our existence today, waiting for God's Word to be spoken. The Spirit is the trigger that activates the creative power of the Word of God. A trigger is a mechanism that discharges a weapon or initiates a device, setting off a chain reaction that results in action and precipitates a series of reactions that explode with force and power. Life and death is in your mouth and what you say is what you get; speak the Word of God and the Word of Life into the circumstances of your life. As you speak the Word of Life, the Holy Spirit plants the creative word into the womb of your existence, a seed that has the power to reproduce itself, just as God's Word has the power to reproduce itself into your life.

John writes that when the Samaritan woman came to draw water, Jesus spoke to her and it was then that her anonymity began to fade. She could not pass the moment on to a surrogate; she had to live the moment for herself. She would either give birth to new possibilities or abort the opportunity. The choice was hers; the choice is yours.

Discipline of the Well

Well Lesson

The first Well Lesson is that living life for and through anyone else but Jesus Christ is an unproductive venture. How can God take you where you have never been before if you allow someone else to take the journey? It's your life—live it!

The second Well Lesson is that you can learn to be your own birth mother by being receptive to the possibilities of God. Spiritual stretch marks are signs of growth. God's Word is the creative seed that initiated creation. It separated land and sea, light and darkness, flinging sun, moon, and stars into their orbits. When God spoke, "Let there be . . ." creation took place (Genesis 1:3). It is in the stretching out on God's Word that our spiritual stretch marks appear. Instead of allowing fear to consume us, we stretch out on God's Word, which grants power, love, and a sound mind (2 Timothy 1:7). Before making up our minds, we can stretch out with God's help by trusting Him and not leaning on our own understanding (Proverbs 3:5–6). Rather than wishing and hoping, we stretch by taking it to the Lord in prayer. We have not because we ask not (James 4:3). We could throw a pity party, but we stretch to have a praise party. All things can work together for good for those who love the Lord and are called according to his purpose (Romans 8:28).

The third Well Lesson is that there is support beyond your human limitations. When life's load is too heavy to carry by yourself, God handles the weight of expanding possibilities and increasing responsibilities. Jesus bears our burdens; we don't need to surrogate life to someone else. There is help when we trust God to strengthen the muscles of our womb. With God's help we can bear the weight of life.

Well Words

Blessed is she who has believed that what the Lord has said to her will be accomplished.

LUKE 1:45

But we have this treasure in jars of clay to show that this all-surpassing power is from God and not from us.

2 CORINTHIANS 4:7

"Woman you have great faith! Your request is granted."

MATTHEW 15:28

"Come with me by yourselves to a quiet place and get some rest."

MARK 6:31

"As a mother comforts her child, so I will comfort you; and you will be comforted . . ."

ISAIAH 66:13

". . . I have come that they may have life, and have it to the full."

JOHN 10:10

I praise you because I am fearfully and wonderfully made . . .

PSALM 139:14

. . . and have put on the new self, which is being renewed in knowledge in the image of its Creator.

COLOSSIANS 3:10

. . . and you have been given fullness in Christ, who is the head over every power and authority.

COLOSSIANS 2:10

Well Sabbatical

⌒ Spend quiet moments meditating upon Luke 1:37: "For nothing is impossible with God."
⌒ What impossible things, fears, and doubts, deny God's possibility for you? Write about it in your journal.

Well Language

⌒ I am pregnant with the possibilities of God.
⌒ I am my own birth mother of my today and tomorrow.
⌒ God is able to handle the weight.
⌒ I am stretching out on the Word of God.
⌒ I can birth new ideas, new dreams, new visions, and new realities.
⌒ When shall we live if not now?
⌒ If there is no enemy within the enemy outside can do us no harm.

Well Work

1. Take a spiritual vitamin daily. A spiritual vitamin is taken by looking up and reading the Scriptures cited in this chapter and others from the Word of God.
2. Purchase a devotional, if you haven't already. Read it daily, perhaps during your sabbatical, to help you dwell on the pure, lovely, honorable, just, and true.

3. Identify one verse that elicits a warm response in you. A verse that makes you smile, encourages your heart, or makes you feel good can become the umbilical cord that nourishes the new life growing in you.

4. In a color you love write on a five-by-seven file card: God is able to carry the weight! Put it on your dresser or bathroom mirror, refrigerator door, or some place where you will see it every day.

5. Work on your collage. Identify those images that represent new possibilities for you. Remember to make room for the new arrival since you are pregnant with the possibilities of God. You could also get balloons in a color you absolutely adore representing areas of concern in your life: home, career, spouse, male relationships, girlfriends, parents, in-laws, and mental and physical health. Stretch the balloons by blowing them up to indicate your expanding capability that God is helping to handle. On the balloon write the changes you are praying for. You may attach them to your collage, but be careful not to break the balloons!

6. Write in your journal the new ideas God is birthing in you.

5

A Woman Breaking
Down Barriers

*The Samaritan woman said to him, "You are a Jew and I am a
Samaritan woman. How can you ask me for a drink?"*

JOHN 4:9

*E*nglish was a second language for Andrina. She had been in the
United States for a month, living with her older sister. She had heard
about freedoms and opportunities, a great melting pot of people from
around the world, and the enormous wealth of America. Enthusiastic
about getting to know her new world she set out each morning to explore her tree-lined city neighborhood. She noticed that the couple next
door seemed to avoid greeting her whenever they passed on the side-
walk. For no apparent reason, they seemed suspicious of her; Andrina
thought maybe it was her imagination, but when she asked her sister
about the couple, her sister explained that not everyone likes people
who are different from them. Andrina was aware that she looked and
sounded different from most people in the neighborhood, but she was
confused because she knew America was built by people who looked
and sounded different from one another. She had come up against an
unexpected barrier.

Have you ever broken through barriers? I felt my shackles release me to my destiny as the new pastor of two small churches in Chesapeake City, Maryland, on the Eastern Shore. It was my second Sunday. The first-Sunday jitters had passed, and as I gazed over the small sanctuary that could only hold forty to fifty people, it seemed everyone in town had come to hear this woman preacher. As I mounted the wooden pulpit, the floor creaked under my weight. I stood before the people in a simple black robe and shepherd's stole. The old piano in the corner cranked out a familiar hymn and the people rose to begin worship as they had done for almost one hundred years. I looked at them as they stood, eyes asking and waiting for something to happen. My voice rose in the proclamation: "This is the day the Lord has made, let us rejoice and be glad in it." I shouted it a second time, and they responded with "amens." The third time I asked them to repeat after me; their voices rose hesitantly at first. But on the fourth time, the whispers became a crescendo as pastor and people united as one voice. It was an exhilarating, liberating moment as I released what I had been born and prepared all my life to do. I felt like a colt being released from the corral without bit or bridle to run free—not wild, but for the first time encountering my call to a precious freedom filled with responsibility and accountability.

Societal prejudices, along with cultural expectations, can have a strong influence on who we become. Accomplishing something when you're being cheered on is one thing; carrying on and moving forward when most people are skeptical or against you is another ball game. The Samaritan woman did not have any cheerleaders to encourage her along the way. She found herself limited within the confines of a society that viewed her as worthless, and she clung desperately to her one hope that one day things would change. She felt trapped within the barriers that limited who she was and who she could become.

We are forever putting walls in place to define the limitations of our space. These walls can be visible, like the walls that divide people, separate nations, and protect environments; or they may be invisible, like the walls that divide genders, separate races, protect prejudices, and define places and possessions for people. This chapter addresses how each of us can empower humanity and ourselves by accepting the challenge in our daily lives to break down barriers by moving beyond the barriers that divide and lessen us. Reach for your higher self!

DIVIDING LIMITATIONS

As a child I attended Robert Brown Elliot School Number 104 Colored School Number Nine. The plaque on the front of the building proclaimed the Robert Brown Elliot part, but the colored school part was carved out of the brick high above the front door, stretching from one end of the building to the other. It was a good school. The teachers and administrators were men and women I saw in church; they lived in neighborhoods like mine, and they were positive and supportive. We knew nothing of society's judgments about who we were, what we could and could not do, and what the future would be. All we knew is that one day all of us were going to college. There was never any other thought drilled into us. Success was education, education was power, and education was the key to a future beyond where your parents lived. College was expected, and there were no exceptions. We learned to recite the poetry of Langston Hughes by heart; we went to hear Marian Anderson in a concert sponsored by Delta Sigma Theta Sorority.

As great as our school was, my father believed it lacked the equipment, space, and other amenities, like musical instruction and a gymnasium, that were abundant in the schools in white neighborhoods. One day my father took me to the principal's office of School Number 60, located on Gwynns Falls Parkway. It was big, fully equipped, and brand new. My father wanted to transfer me to this school in a white neighborhood, and he wanted to register me right then, but the principal refused. My father asked me to read from one of the books in the office, and I did. He asked me to write about what I had just read, and he asked the principal to give me math problems to see my proficiency; he then asked the principal to give me some spelling words. The principal was not very impressed. He looked across what appeared to me to be the biggest desk in the world; his look made me feel so small and insignificant that I knew that even if he could, he was not going to let me attend his new school.

The Samaritan woman faced prejudice through a patriarchal system that kept women essentially silent and secluded, their heads and faces covered. Whether a woman lived in Rome, Greece, Jerusalem, or Samaria, her status in the community was basically the same. A woman was a second-class citizen valued as an asset in procreation and home management, but largely thought of as a liability to be protected and provided for. The Samaritan woman didn't have what we consider in this generation "rights," and in her era, "privileges." A woman rarely worked outside the home, her opinions were not sought, and her views were not valued. Women did not receive formal education, yet were responsible for the early education of their children. Women prepared the meals, but were not allowed to eat with guests. Conversations between men and women were discouraged. Women were not allowed to work or earn income and therefore mere survival demanded they have a man. They were bought or sold, married or divorced at the will of their husbands or fathers. The participation of women in Judaic religious life during the Old and New Testament times was only marginal. Women's natural bodily functions regularly disqualified them from worship, for menstruating women were considered ritually unclean and unworthy to be in the presence of God. They were not required to make pilgrimages to Jerusalem for the major festivals or to study the Torah; and recitation by them of mealtime prayers was not permitted. Women were not even counted in the minyan, which was the quorum of persons needed for worship to take place. In theory, any adult could read or preach in the synagogue. In practice, however, women and men were physically separate during worship.

The Authorized Daily Prayer Book, used by worshipers in the Jerusalem temple, revealed one of the prevailing attitudes about women: The men blessed God in their prayers for not creating them women and the women blessed God for creating them according to Divine will. In the rabbinic tradition, only boys were taught and trained to be rabbis. Women were excluded, though a few rabbis ignored the tradition and taught their daughters the Torah anyway. Philo, a Jewish philosopher, believed women were evil and inferior. Jewish historian Josephus also believed in the theoretical inferiority of women, but mentions a number of influential women in his writings. Although women were considered inferior and subservient, some emerged as leaders making contributions to their community and God's plan of salvation. In spite of the general societal limitations and the dim view of women's skills, ancient Judaic communities were willing to acknowledge individual women whose gifts and charisma could not be denied. Women such as Miriam, Anna, Huldah, Noadiah, and the wife of Isaiah were prophets. Deborah was a judge and Esther was a queen and heroine. New Testament exceptions include the four daughters of Philip, who prophesied; Mary, the mother of Jesus; Mary Magdalene; and Priscilla, who pastored a church with her husband, Aquila. Though her name was not recorded and though she did not have an official "call," this Samaritan woman was also an exception, evangelizing Sychar.

It hurts when the door is closed in your face, acceptance denied, just because you are a woman. It hurts when the door is closed in your face, acceptance denied, just because of the color of your skin. Sometimes it feels we are all too good at building barriers and walls, setting boundaries that separate us from ourselves, our loved ones, the communities and countries surrounding us. The walls of Jerusalem protected the city from the violence of man and animals. But the walls of a sanctuary can become confining. The Great Wall of China, started in the third century B.C., kept invaders out and the Chinese in. The Berlin Wall, built at the close of World War II, divided east from west, communism from democracy, sisters, lovers, family, and friends. Jesus was leaning against the walls of Jacob's well, hot from the heat, weary from the walk and very thirsty. Yet he was also leaning against the walls of a history, culture, and society older than the walls of Jacob's well.

When Andrina realized the people in her new neighborhood wouldn't speak to her or look at her at least in part because she was different, it's understandable that she was frustrated. She couldn't believe it. Sure, she was the new kid on the block, but hadn't everyone in her neighborhood been new at one time? She began to feel belittled, which made her more frustrated, even angry. The more she thought about the situation the more frustrated she became.

Everyone has been frustrated at some time—having a complete sense of dissatisfaction that comes with having unresolved issues, the feeling that comes from unfulfilled needs, the sting that smarts the face while life tosses up yet another rejection. It comes when doors are slammed, gates shut, and brick walls are erected where you thought a main thoroughfare would take you up the yellow brick road of success. Frustration knows your first, middle, and last name and it will call you in and out trying to drive you out of your right mind. Frustration knows where you live, eats at your dinner table, and tries to spend as many nights with you as possible. Frustration will tuck you in bed at night, help you say your prayers, and when you toss and turn in your sleep, frustration will tell you that there is no point in trying to sleep because it is almost dawn. When God's grace awakens you to a new day and mercy pulls you from a prone to a perpendicular position, frustration will get you your morning newspaper, pour you a cup of hot coffee, bring you juice, kiss you good-bye on the cheek, and tell you to have a nice day. Frustration will get under your skin and keep you talking to yourself while stopping you from talking to others. Frustration can and will keep you off balance, disturb your concentration, cloud your vision, and destroy your faith. Frustration does have its limitations; it can't kill you, but it can make you want to die.

One of the greatest sources of frustration for women is when doors of opportunity close. Closed not because they're incompetent, ignorant, untrained, unskilled, unprepared or stupid; not because they're Asian, African American, Hispanic, Native American, or Caucasian, but because they're female. Doors are closed because of gender, and if by chance a woman happens to get in, limitations are placed upon her upward mobility. That's frustration.

Perhaps you have experienced this frustration. Some doors are closed because of the color of your skin. Other doors are shut because of your nationality or your socioeconomic status. Frustration is greatest when a member of your own family, or gender, or heritage closes the door. It hurts when someone you've worked with side by side, bloodied and unbowed, fighting to obtain some measure of evenhandedness at great price—someone with whom you've protested, picketed, signed petitions for change, and struggled for equality, justice, and fair play—slams the door in your face. It hurts when the door slammers share the same history or the same hue. It hurts when they've also tasted the bitter waters of segregation and faced the "colored-only" restrooms, parks, swimming pools, and housing. When they have also known the anger of corporate rejection, felt the sting of a national policy of exclusion, known what it's like to be denied, pushed to the back of the buses of American life, or to the end of the line. When they've known what it's like to be blamed for everything—you're to blame for crime, violence, drugs, poverty, welfare, affirmative action, or teenage pregnancy. Life in America would be a whole lot better if you and your kind were not around.

Daughters learn from their elders that the door should be avoided; they learn that it may never open, so don't even try. Instead of walking through any door to any career, women were steered toward careers that centered on the care and nurturing of others. They trained for the so-called feminine professions of teaching, nursing, and social work and were prepared to leave those when they married. Other women were sent to college, not to learn and achieve and become successful, but to find husbands. Girls and women are taught to hold back, not to run as hard or as far or as fast, not to play as rough, not to be as smart, bright, or brilliant, not to be so good that they will be unattractive to men. Frustration is closing the door in your own face because you think your gifts and talents make you unattractive to a man and for the sake of appearances you are careful not to walk through the door first.

Although the view of ancient Hebrew women could be summed up in the words "suppressed," "secluded," and "silent," the situation was very different for ancient African women. African society in antiquity did not view or treat women as helpless, emotional, and inferior appendages. They did not view their men as strong, adventuresome, and aggressive superiors. Traditional African communities considered both genders as vital participants in society. Men and women worked side by side in their respective groups, communities, and associations. Men were rulers, warriors, religious leaders, educators, and kingdom builders. African cave art depicts women not only in maternal and domestic roles, but also as warriors and artisans. Women were equal partners in community building. They were ritual leaders whose gifts, talents, and influence were essential to the life of their communities.

In order for a community to be strong it needs the participation of both men and women. You cannot be strong by making the other weak. A community will never be strong as long as there's only one part functioning in the relationship. Our community's shame has been allowing division between the genders by pitting one against the other. It fragments our efforts because we fail to recognize that it takes two to tango. A house divided cannot stand.

Dividing walls tend to create fear rather than build trust. The dividing walls in the Samaritan woman's life were so great that she was afraid of the valley she found herself in. As she clung to her one last hope, and in spite of her fears, she kept going to fetch water every day. The psalmist writes, Even though I walk through the valley of the shadow of death, I will fear no evil . . . (Psalm 23:4). He did not say even though I stand, sit, or camp out in the valley. The verse indicates motion. Even though I walk through the shadow, and the appearance of a deadly experience, I will not fear evil. Even though I face sexism, racism, classism, and my own past mistakes, I will keep walking, I will fear no evil. The valley experience is a walk-through, not a place of permanent habitation. Too often we slip into the habit of just staying in the valley. These are habits we need to slip out of, and find new ones we should slip into. Slip out of procrastination and slip into discipline. Slip out of starting and not finishing and slip into completing. Slip out of childish attitudes and slip into maturity. Slip out of spending what you don't have and slip into fiscal responsibility. Slip out of self-hatred and slip into a healthy self-esteem. We need to slip out of racism, slip out of sexism, slip out of male bashing, and slip out of every other exclusionary ism that embarrasses the Gospel of Jesus Christ. We can slip out of stereotyping, the habit that lumps everyone together and judges and condemns everybody based upon hearsay or one negative experience. Well-meaning people say "All blacks..." "All Hispanics..." "All Koreans..." "All women do this..." "All churches do that..." Let us slip out of negativity and a vocabulary filled with no, can't, never, not now, and impossible. There is nothing wrong with acknowledging negativity, but don't live negatively for the rest of your life. Negativity plays an important part in life, functioning as an early warning system of impending danger. It warns us to slow down when we need to examine deeper, move cautiously, or take notice of what's going on in our bodies or lives. But negativity can also be a wall separating us from our higher selves—the ones Christ is challenging and helping us to attain.

OUR HIGHER SELVES

As I mention in my book *Not Without a Struggle,* I was appointed to a historic congregation in Baltimore, Payne Memorial AME Church, in 1990. I was the first woman to shepherd that congregation and the first woman assigned to a church of that size and heritage. Bishop H. Hartford Brookings, then the presiding prelate of the second Episcopal District, where Payne Memorial was located, asked me if I could handle the appointment. He said that my failure would not just be my personal failure; it would mean that a woman would not be appointed to such a charge for a very long time. My success could open the door for other women to follow. It meant that once again, I would have to carry the load not just of my people, but also of all my sisters, just to do what God had called me to do. Every time I mounted that pulpit, stood to teach Bible study, held the young to baptize them into the faith, or the old as they slipped from this life, judgment would not only be passed on me, but also on all other women called to do the same. Now, as the first elected and consecrated bishop in the AME church's 214-year history who happens to be a woman, I carry not only the burden to do what God called me to do on a greater personal level, but also for the other women who are coming quickly behind me.

People had doubts about whether I could do it. Jesus told me, "I can do everything through him who gives me strength" (Philippians 4:13). The world wanted me to stick to what was expected of me. God's Word tells me "I am fearfully and wonderfully made" (Psalm 139:14). The world wanted me to prove that I am worthy, but Jesus tells me "whosoever calls upon the name of the Lord shall be saved" (Romans 10:13) and to walk worthy of our calling. The world wanted me to live within its programmed prejudices, but the Word of God tells me "there is neither Greek nor Jew, slave nor free, male nor female, for you are all one in Christ Jesus" (Galatians 3:28). The world wanted me to live in my assigned place in the back of the bus, at the rear where brotherhood must be legislated and praxis never catches up to policy, but the Word of God tells me that I am more than a conqueror (Romans 8:37). The world would have me silent as a lamb led to the slaughter, but the Word tells me your sons and daughters shall prophesy (Joel 2:28, Acts 2). I didn't set out to break any barriers and I had no intention of stepping out of the corner designated for my gender. I resisted as hard as I could the irrepressible urge to drop my mundane water pots and go to the city to tell them about Jesus and this well. The world had nothing to tell me except what I could not do and who I could not be.

Jesus comes to the well and breaks all the rules. He speaks to the woman at the well, he grants her attention, he treats her with dignity, he acknowledges her value, and he gives purpose, meaning, and assignment to her life. Jesus is still doing that for all who come to the well. Jesus engages in a relationship beyond the cultural and societal dictates.

I was born in a world defined by barriers. Not defined by me or my ancestors, with us in mind, but within the limitations of the culture's idea of who I and my people are. I exist in a limited environment that ever seeks to build new plantations for the enslaved. In the past, it was sharecropping that kept people down on the farm, today it is the minimum wage. It used to be physical enslavement, now it is the enslaved mind that acts out dysfunctional behavior in its self-destructive appetite that destroys itself so that others do not have to. It used to be physical chains that bind; now the chains of ignorance and apathy are a legacy inherited.

Jesus addresses the questions of ethnic racism and gender issues at the well with the Samaritan woman. Since the time that Jacob bought the ground upon which the well was dug, hundreds of years of bitterness and hatred between the Jews and the Samaritans had passed. Jesus unexpectedly begins talking with a Samaritan woman at this historically significant well, and he breaks down two barriers. The first barrier is racism: the wall erected between the Jews and Samaritans. Nearly four hundred years of bitterness washed away the moment Jesus talked to the woman at the well. When Jesus spoke to her, he took the sting out of the rejection that Samaritans had suffered at the hands of the Jews because they could not prove their genealogy and purity of their race. Arguments over whether the holy writing was just the Pentateuch (the first five books of the Hebrew Bible), or the Torah, were not raised. Questions over whether they worshiped in Jerusalem or at Mount Gerazim were not yet raised. When he spoke to the woman at the well the air became pregnant with a new understanding between Jews and Samaritans.

The second barrier is sexism: the walls between men and women. The woman at the well was concerned, but not alarmed, about this man at her well. The cut of his robe and the weave of the material revealed that he was Jewish, a rabbi perhaps. Men didn't publicly speak to women, especially Jewish men to Samaritan women, but now the silence was broken. It was as if the air stopped moving, the sun paused in its rotation, and thousands of years of social tradition came to attention. You could almost hear him saying, love the Lord with all your heart, mind, and strength; and love your neighbor as yourself. There is more going on here than "Hello, I need a drink of water." Jesus is plowing new ground for all our relationships. He is introducing a new paradigm for relationships between Jews and Samaritans, and men and women. Jesus breaks through the barrier of prejudice when he stops to talk and listen to a woman. He is announcing that your reasons for excluding your neighbor are no longer valid and your previous discriminatory and exclusionary philosophies will no longer hold water. His words interrupted her day and demanded a response. It is true that day at the well, and true today; the Words of Christ still demand a response.

Jesus was introducing inclusion as a way of life. Inclusion had nothing to do with history as Jews and Samaritans; arguments over history, heritage, and gender would no longer divide people. In speaking to her that day at the well, Jesus announced that their differences no longer mattered; centuries of venom and hatred melted in the hot desert sun as he said, "I'm thirsty and want something to drink." What a cataclysmic encounter. History was being made, the threads of argument, prejudice, and racism were unraveling, and the justification for building walls that divide was being shaken. Sameness was in trouble. She was amazed that he spoke to her as he leaned against the well and she said, "How do you speak to me a Samaritan and you a Jew?" It is the same way we think in our minds, and sometimes say aloud, "How do you speak to me? I'm a Korean and you're African American." "How do you speak to me? I'm Hispanic and you're Aborigine." "How do you speak to me? I'm Asian and you're Native American?" "Why do you speak to me? I'm urban and you are suburban." "How do you speak to me when I'm country and you're city, when I'm rich and you're poor, when I'm old money and you're nouveau riche, when I'm a baby boomer and you're generation X, Y, or Z?" We have been all too busy building walls, separating ourselves by color, dollar signs, pedigree, and petty arguments. When Jesus said "hello" at the well, he was opening a door, and introducing us to the universality of his message. It was a foreshadowing of the work of the cross.

In the Christian tradition, before the cross, specific barriers clouded relationships between God and his people. The Old Testament indicates that in order to worship one must be ritually clean. Women during their regular menses were barred from worship. Ritual purity and racial purity were of significant value then. After the cross, the racial and gender barriers to worship came to an end. As Paul writes in Galatians 3:28, "There is neither Jew nor Greek, slave nor free, male nor female, for you are all one in Christ Jesus." The dividing walls that separated groups from God and from one another fell when Christ was nailed to the cross. The paradigm of inclusion rose with Christ from the grave on the morning of the Resurrection. In the Acts of the Apostles, the Bible shows the growth of the church after the Resurrection from a national concern to an international one. The early Christian community consisted primarily of a Judaic constituency, spread to the Gentiles and then others as Jesus demonstrated the inclusive nature of God at the well. He de-emphasized racial and ethnic origins. He died for all.

Andrina and her sister were frustrated, but they decided to try to break through their frustration by going next door to introduce themselves. At first they were scared and wondered if it was such a good idea. When they knocked on the door and the woman answered, she seemed surprised to see them standing on the front step. Quickly, Andrina's sister introduced herself and Andrina, pointing out that they lived next door and thought it would be nice to know a neighbor. The woman's face softened. She seemed pleased and called her husband from the other room to come meet the neighbors.

Integration arrived in Baltimore as I entered the sixth grade, and I was bused to School number 18 on a hill in the Park Heights area of the city. The school year began with a season of culture shock. My, how things had changed. I remember telling my parents after the first week of school that I wasn't sure I liked this new world. The people talked funny and they were not positive or receptive to our presence in the school. The teachers were no longer supportive; they had little expectation for our achievement. They seemed surprised when we managed to get good grades, even the highest in the class. I told my parents that I felt it was my duty to prove every day that I had a right to be there. And I did.

The Samaritan woman needed a breakthrough. The women of this ancient culture and all of the Samaritans needed a breakthrough and she, of all people, became a breakthrough for them and many others. She was a woman down to her last things carrying a pot of one hope. She had no idea that she was a pioneer, the first woman Jesus publicly spoke to, and the first Samaritan he had engaged in a relationship with. Later, she would become the first person he told about his Messiahship. In ancient Palestine, the identities of Hebrew women were tied to the productiveness of their wombs and their marital status. Necessity is the mother of invention. Rosa Parks needed to sit down after a long day at work. The only seats available on the bus were in the front. The colored seats were in the back. From this necessity and her courage in standing her ground, the Civil Rights Movement was born. The Samaritan woman needed water and her humanity was affirmed. Jesus spoke, and the walls of the Hebrew patriarchal society where women were not treated as people, but chattel, cracked. Jesus asked a question of a woman in public when not even a husband would speak publicly to his wife. She was startled by the conversation. This was not going to be an ordinary day at the well.

A religious group of Pharisees in Palestine considered themselves so pious they closed their eyes when they saw a woman walking down the street. They did not want to look upon anyone who did not have a soul. They were called in some literature the wall-bumping rabbis because when they closed their eyes they would bump into walls. Jesus spoke beyond tradition, culture, gender, and law to affirm the Samaritan woman. He validated her personhood. Jesus probably did not care what others would think. He did not care about the criticisms of the Pharisees or the Jewish religious leaders when he healed a woman on the Sabbath. When he stood strong in the midst of an angry crowd to take the side of an adulterous woman, he was not stopped by what people thought. Jesus faced criticism from those who wondered why a holy man took his meals with sinners and wine bibbers. He told stories with a Samaritan as the hero, took time to pull children onto his lap, touch lepers, and talk to women in public. His concern was to do what is right and he was willing to break through the lines of tradition, race, and gender to speak to this well woman. He chose to rise above exclusionary thinking. Attending integrated schools in the 1960s was not an easy thing. There were people like the principal in Gwynns Falls Parkway, so pious, pretending not to see what was going on, closing his eyes to racism like the wall-bumping rabbis. Being the first female bishop has its challenges. With opportunity comes responsibility and with that duty comes joy. Being the first at anything, especially where gender and race are involved, calls for strength, grace, and flexibility.

The heat of opposition and the heat of the day may cause you to fade in the noon sun. Put on Son block. We are more than conquerors (Romans 8:37). There is an old song that I love in our hymnal that says, "I'm pressing on the upward way; new heights I'm gaining every day; still praying as I'm onward bound, plant my feet on higher ground." At this well, Jesus speaks to our higher self. He calls us up a little higher, out of our prejudicial attitudes and gender biases to the well. He calls us to include what others have excluded for generations. It was not an ordinary day at the well. The Samaritan woman was engaged in a conversation of historical and theological consequence. Jesus put a crack in the dividing walls separating Jews and Samaritans, and men and women. The visible signs of crumbling still continue through to our generation of well women. There are some things we must never forget. Our Jewish friends do not want us ever to forget the Holocaust and our Native American friends may not want us to forget Wounded Knee. To forget is to create the environment for it to happen again, to lose the lessons learned from mistakes of the past. To forget is to diminish the pain of the experience, dismiss the suffering of those maligned, misused, or misjudged. To forget is to condone the behavior of those who should be embarrassed for their actions, not to mention all the societal and cultural limitations that permit prejudice and fear, and produce policy and practice of the most obscene and horrendous sort.

The plight of this well woman and her twenty-first-century sisters is real. Disregard for her personhood, disrespect for her femininity, distrust of her actions, displeasure in her presence, dislike of her assertive proclamation of the Messiah's coming. "Dis" is a negative addition to a word that has a positive meaning. A woman who is created in the image of God, just like her brothers, often carries negative baggage of a sexist and racist and classist society. But, we must always remember, "God saw all that he had made, and it was very good," (Genesis 1:31). I share these things not to merely go over old ground or to make anyone uncomfortable, but because it is a part of her story. It is a history that informs the Samaritan woman's present and has a determining effect upon her future. It is a part of my story, a history that informs my present and impacts my future. The Samaritans and the Jews were programmed to hate one another. Their conflict was validated by sacred writ, centuries of bitterness passed from one generation to the next. It was celebrated, sung, and passed from the eldest to the youngest, continuing the prejudice. The prejudices of both groups were the canvass upon which their encounter at Jacob's well took place. Their conversation changed the picture of programmed prejudice and foreshadowed the beloved community John was heralding.

CALL TO ACTION

Well women do not hide behind other people's behavior when they reject justice and fair play. Ask yourself, "What does the Bible teach us to do?" It says we are all one in Christ Jesus, we are to love our neighbors, not to think of ourselves more highly than we ought, and not to judge each other. Do these things. If your friends do not want to speak to "them," you speak. If your coworkers do not want to work with "them," you work. If your family does not want to support you in doing good things in your community, then do it alone. Like Jesus, we can extend ourselves beyond the ordinary to reach people, becoming out-of-the-ordinary people in out-of-the-way places. The easy and ordinary way beckons regularly, but we must meet the challenge of taking a different and less frequently traveled pathway. The conversation at the well was a foretaste of the work of the cross and the resurrection. Jesus was preparing the disciples and us for what was to come in the upper room, in the garden, at the tomb, at the resurrection, at the ascension, at the Pentecost, and on the missionary journey. Jesus was showing how it ought to be among nations, cultures, and peoples speaking to all of us when he spoke to this woman. He broke down barriers in preparation for a glorious work of salvation. If the Lord did not exclude the Samaritan woman, he is not about to exclude you. An old song sung in churches for generations states it like this: "There is no secret what God can do. What He's done for others, He'll do for you." When we are faced with cultural habits, approaches to life, and prejudices that hem us in, take a page from the story of the Samaritan woman who went to Jacob's well. There is healing power in the spirit of Jesus' love. Opportunities may fade, but God has the power to create them. Doors may close, but God can open them. When the old boy or old girl network tries to chew you up, remember the network of God the Father, the Son, and the Holy Spirit. It is tempting to build walls of your own to keep things out, but they also keep you in. We have allowed our eyes to be blinded by color, dollar signs, pedigree, petty arguments, and other stereotypes. There are old habits we need to slip out of and new habits we should slip into. Jesus sets the example for us to move forward even without the help or approval of others. When Jesus said "hello" at the well, he was opening the door and introducing us to the universality of his message: Love one another unconditionally.

Discipline of the Well

Well Lesson

Breakthrough women, the first lesson from the well is that the petty distinctions of race and gender used to divide kingdoms and communities are not valid in the eyes of God. Jesus becomes a catalyst for change, upsetting our set of beliefs, attitudes, assumptions, and expectations. The Divine tells us to throw aside these skin-color differences, hair-type differences, where-you're-born differences. With a simple "hello" at the well we are encouraged to slip out from where we are, and slip into what we were created to be, neither Greek nor Jew, bond nor free, male nor female—we are all one in Christ Jesus (Galatians 3:28). The Samaritan woman needed water to survive, but Jesus startled her by affirming her humanity.

The second Well Lesson is that Jesus sets an example for us to move forward and break down barriers even without the help, support, or approval of others. Jesus came to the well and broke all the rules as he spoke to a woman, acknowledged her value, talked with her with integrity and purpose, and he will do the same for us if we'll let him. The Samaritan woman overcame being a second-class citizen, racism, gender bias, rejection of a patriarchal system, and she became an evangelist before her time. Follow the example of Jesus and the Samaritan woman.

The third Well Lesson is to be a breakthrough woman by applying God's grace and inclusion to everyday, ordinary situations, letting our higher self break down barriers. When frustration hits you in the face, reach for your higher self. Jesus can give spiritual perspective and lift anyone above the narrow-minded interpretation of a community or person whose mindset tries to keep you from drinking deeply from the well of Living Water. Drop your pots and take a message to the people. "I can do everything through him who gives me strength" (Philippians 4:13).

Well Words

To do what is right and just is more acceptable to the Lord than sacrifice.

PROVERBS 21:3

. . . who shows no partiality to princes and does not favor the rich over the poor, for they are all the work of his hands?

JOB 34:19

Then Peter began to speak: "I now realize how true it is that God does not show favoritism . . ."

ACTS 10:34

There is no difference between Jew and Gentile—the same Lord is Lord of all and richly blesses all who call on him . . .

ROMANS 10:12

Defend the cause of the weak and fatherless; maintain the rights of the poor and oppressed.

PSALM 82:3

Well Sabbatical

- In your quiet time, meditate on two scriptures: Psalm 139 and Galatians 3:28.

- Be still. Focus your thoughts upon how fearfully and wonderfully you are made in the image of God.

- Pray this prayer: "My God, I come to you today knowing that I was intentionally created. If anyone makes the mistake of excluding me, Jesus, include me. In Jesus name, Amen."

Well Language

— *My uniqueness does not mean I am inferior or superior. It means I am unique.*

— *Look for the best in everyone.*

— *Do not exclude what God includes.*

— *My freedom does not require the enslavement of another human.*

— *I will not allow other people's prejudices to create obstacles for me.*

— *I am loved. I am wanted. I belong. (Put hand over heart and repeat.)*

Well Work

1. *Read biographies of women from cultures other than your own.*

2. *Study a culture different from your own.*

3. *Learn to say a few words or phrases from a different language.*

4. *Rent a video such as:* Schindler's List, Amistad, Philadelphia, West Side Story, *or* Shogun. *Put yourself in the shoes of those who were excluded. How do you think it felt? How would you behave differently?*

5. *Write in your journal about prejudicial feelings you have against a person or a group. Pray and ask God to help you overcome these feelings.*

6

A Woman Overcomes
Learned Ignorance

~~~~~~

*Jesus answered her, "If you knew the gift of God and who it is that
asks you for a drink, you would have asked him and
he would have given you living water."*

JOHN 4:10

In the beginning, Jerry shared with me, he hadn't minded driving
his wife everywhere. They enjoyed this nice and cozy time together in the car. Now they have children who have their own schedules,
his wife works outside the home, his job is on the opposite side of town,
and what was nice and cozy has become an inconvenience. Jerry has
tried everything to get his wife to learn how to drive. He paid for lessons;
she didn't take them. He bought her a car; she doesn't drive it. He set
aside money for gas and car upkeep; the money is still in the bank. His
wife has no physical impairment that prevents her from learning how
to drive. She simply desires to remain ignorant of how to drive an automobile.

When my husband and I moved into a detached home several
years ago, a few shade trees and lots of grass surrounded it—grass that
needed to be cut. Stan purchased a state-of-the-art gas lawn mower with

111

a grass catcher on the side. It was a beautiful green machine that purred when started. In early spring, the grass grew like tall weeds. My husband intended to teach me how to use his green machine so I could help him with the grass-cutting chores. I made it clear that I did not want to learn how to work his green machine, where to put the gasoline, or how to empty the clippings. Why? I wanted to remain ignorant about cutting grass with a power mower because I did not ever want to be asked to do such a thing. I could have leaned on learned ignorance and practiced learned helplessness for the rest of my life. Eventually, however, I rose above my laziness, stubbornness, and dodging my grass-cutting responsibilities. Now, in the absence of teenagers and husband, I can be pressed into service, if necessary.

The Samaritan woman couldn't or wouldn't see that maybe there was a way out of the lifestyle she had come to know all too well. Five failed marriages and a frowned-upon current relationship gave her something to hide out about. Still, she did have one hope that one day things would change, and she kept going to the well to fetch water. She may have felt down, she may have felt angry or ashamed, but she got up and went to the well. She took a risk and spoke to Jesus. And that changed everything. She went from being a woman carrying empty vessels, a woman whose life was mired in failure and isolation, to becoming a woman of belief, of action, of value. She became herself a vessel filled and overflowing with Good News.

Oftentimes, like the woman at the well, we are programmed to believe we can or cannot do something. In chapter six, we see that the Samaritan woman learns that she has been responding to her programmed expectations about life, and that in order for things to one day change, she must risk the challenge of changing herself. We all have the option of holding on to the learned ignorance in our lives—whether we believe we can't possibly balance a checkbook, run a mile, write a résumé, or help a child with her math problems—or we have the option of taking the risk to change our behavior and fulfill the potential of our lives. We have choices to make—informed choices. Ignorance is not bliss. Rise up beyond ignorance and become a well woman!

THINK YOU CAN? THINK YOU CAN'T?

Learned ignorance is a crutch that some people use: They deliberately appear ignorant or helpless when they are not. They think the same way they've always thought or think the same way the people around them think because it's easier than thinking for themselves. Learned helplessness, a kissing cousin of learned ignorance, does not mean that a person is incapable; it means she does not want to do it on her own. If you are legitimately helpless because of health, body, mind, or age, then that is a difficult challenge and not the kind of helplessness we are speaking of here.

Many women spend their lives in learned ignorance, the deliberate decision not to know, not to respond, not to avail themselves of knowledge and information. Learned ignorance leads to intentionally ignoring invitations and opportunities, the too convenient excuse for wasted intellect, skills, and talent. Women who practice learned ignorance are content to exist in narrow worlds of their own making, raising ignorance to an art form acceptable in many social circles. Learned ignorance is much more than never reading the newspaper or a book, and it is more than refusing to work on a computer, deal with the World Wide Web, do e-mail, and stay informed on current events and issues in the information age. It is the refusal to take full accountability and responsibility for your life. It means preferring to remain ignorant about something because, "If I am ignorant, I cannot be held responsible." That's why I didn't want to learn how to run the lawn mower. If I couldn't control the big green machine, it couldn't control me either, and I wouldn't have to be responsible for it. In the end, I decided to be responsible to my family and to myself.

Learned ignorance does not appear suddenly. It is an attitude developed after failed attempts to capitalize on knowledge and information. Remember the women who are adept at living anonymously, the wallpaper women who lack their own structures but can decorate surfaces with their designs? As we have said before, these are the background women who are everybody's support team, power behind the throne, bridesmaid at every wedding, and the midwife of every possibility. For a wallpaper woman, being the birth mother of her own potential and possibilities is not even an option in her mind.

Some of us may be using learned ignorance in one or two areas of our lives, but some of us may be almost paralyzed by it. The fear of learning, the fear of growing, and the fear of success and failure can isolate you from your well-woman potential. The "I can't" and the "I won't" become building blocks for the walls that surround you. You may view them as walls of protection from the stress, anxiety, and challenges of change, but others view your walls of learned ignorance as bars of self-imprisonment around you. Learned ignorance means that the knowing has become a burden rather than a blessing. Ignorance has become the safe harbor of unenlightened retreat. Knowing often opens doors to greater responsibilities that require new skills. Knowing opens the door to unexplored environments; new arenas require that we develop a pioneering spirit, a spirit that will quench our fears, worries, and doubts.

Learned ignorance and learned helplessness drag us down when we start using them to keep us from doing the things we are capable of. Doing what? Doing things such as going back to school, completing a degree, starting your business, writing, reading, joining a club, providing community service, fighting for a cause, going to the physician, learning to drive a car, moving out of your mother's house, and not driving your father's car. Learned helplessness can be much more convenient than self-sufficiency or independence, because once we think "I've got learned helplessness," then there is no need to expend energy when you can get someone else to do it, no need to risk the unknown, paralyze the ego, no need to wrestle with change and challenges when you can let others take care of things. Learned helplessness is a clever cover for cloaking laziness and stubbornness. Learned helplessness is often learned at home, from parents or the significant adults who surrounded you during the tender years of maturation. It's great having parents who do everything for you, until you're grown and on your own and unable to do anything for yourself. It's wonderful having adults who give you everything, until you realize you have no idea how to get anything for yourself. It's marvelous always being on the receiving end, until it's time for you to give. Suddenly, you realize that you don't know how to give support, love, time, attention, or yourself.

Learned ignorance and learned helplessness extend beyond yard work. They extend to every part of our lives. Unfortunately, they are often reinforced by our culture. A young daughter may not realize she is picking up learned ignorance when her mother tells her, "It's okay if you don't understand those math problems. I didn't get math either. It's really for boys." She's learning learned ignorance, not math, when in fact, she could learn math just fine with the right teacher or curriculum. Other people know intellectually they should change a behavior, but it's just easier not to. Sameness can be comforting. There's no risk of conflict, no unknown dangers. Sameness keeps things status quo. Confronting sameness often means work, responsibility, or other unknowns that might shake things up. When a man practices learned helplessness, he can marry a woman who will do hard things for him. If that doesn't work, he can always count on his mother to carry the load for him until death do them part.

The Samaritan woman's learned helplessness and ignorance were reinforced by her culture. She lived at a time when the transfer of knowledge was primarily a male responsibility. Women gave their children early instruction at home, but fathers and other male teachers outside the family continued the children's education. Women were silent and secluded. If a woman wanted to expand her knowledge in animal husbandry, she couldn't. If she wanted to become a money changer, she couldn't. If she wanted to learn the Torah, she was forbidden. Learned helplessness is also a by-product of low self-esteem. If you believe you can't, you won't. If you believe you're not smart, you never will be. If you believe you're not good enough, deserving enough, thin enough, cute enough, loveable enough, you will spend entirely too much time incapacitating your capabilities. It is called learned helplessness.

Words can be a deadly weapon in the mouth of a family member when directed toward a trusting child. A constant barrage of negatives can damage emerging egos, personalities, and attitudes. Can you imagine constantly being told what you cannot do, cannot think, and cannot achieve? Words can be deadly in the hands of culture and society. A person's self-esteem can be eroded by a steady stream of verbal garbage pronouncing you cannot because you are a man, a woman, black, white, immigrant, harlot, druggie, or because God said so. Listen to the language that shapes learned helplessness: "You'll never amount to anything." "You will grow up to be just like your no-good mother, father, sister, brother, or some other black sheep in the family." "I don't know why you're going to try that, you won't make it." "How many times are you going to fail before you quit?" "Who would want to go out with you?" "You can't do that by yourself." "Ask for help next time, and you'll have less problems." "You always make a mess of everything."

Some women practice learned helplessness when faced with automotive challenges, financial challenges, living alone, or something different and challenging in their lives. Every time Cynthia decides to move out of her mother's house and live on her own, her mother becomes helpless. All of a sudden she forgets how to do things she has done for years. She can't go to the supermarket, cleaners, doctor, or dentist without Cynthia. As long as Cynthia is living at home, mother is fine, but as soon as she talks about leaving, her mother becomes helpless. She uses learned helplessness to control the relationship.

Jerry's wife confides to friends that she likes not knowing how to drive; it keeps Jerry close. He must always be a telephone call away so he can take her and pick her up from everything and everywhere. She uses her learned ignorance to control Jerry and their relationship. She has convinced herself that not changing, not learning to drive, gives her more power. Her refusing to learn to drive has become manipulation. She's listening to her culture tell her what she's capable of, she's listening to her fears and neediness. She's hiding behind learned ignorance and learned helplessness, and she and her relationship with her husband are both losing because of it.

RISK

The enemy of learned ignorance is risk. Risk gets sick every time learned ignorance initiates another member to its sorority. Risk means seeking knowledge and using knowledge, not hiding behind ignorance. Risk takes courage; it means doing, going, working, seeing, touching, and feeling in spite of the burden of the blessing.

A response to learned ignorance is summed up in a poem by anonymous. This poem sat on the desk of the former executive director of our nonprofit corporation, Marilyn Aklin. She gave me a copy that now sits on my desk. It challenges learned ignorance.

Risk

To Laugh Is to Risk Appearing the Fool.
To Weep Is to Risk Appearing the Sentimental.
To Reach Out for Another Is to Risk Involvement.
To Expose Feelings Is to Risk Exposing Your True Self.
To Place Your Ideas, Your Dreams, Before a Crowd Is to Risk
Their Loss.
To Love Is to Risk Not Being Loved in Return.
To Live Is to Risk Dying, to Hope Is to Risk Despair.
To Try Is to Risk Failure.
But Risks Must Be Taken, Because the Greatest Hazard in Life Is
to Risk
Nothing.
The Person Who Risks Nothing, Does Nothing, Has Nothing,
and Is
Nothing.
They May Avoid Suffering and Sorrow, but They Cannot Learn,
Feel,

Change, Grow, Love, Live.
Only a Person Who Risks Is Free.
—*Author Unknown*

If I live with risk, I feel that, in spite of the newness, in spite of the unfamiliarity, in spite of the weight of knowing, I am determined to move forward. I don't know everything, but I am willing to try to shoulder the responsibility of knowing. Knowing can be an overwhelming experience. A knowing overload can thrust you into learned ignorance when confronted with too much information, too many details, too many facts, too many alternatives, and too much data to handle. A little bit of knowledge is just as dangerous as too much knowledge. All book sense and no common sense, makes no sense. Pursuing knowledge for the sake of knowledge without applying the knowledge to life is a trap too. This knowledge trap can be used as an excuse, however, for settling for the belief that ignorance is bliss. Many women like it that way. Who can ask you if everyone knows you do not know? Who can count on you, when you consistently remove yourself from center stage? Who seeks you out, when you constantly step out? What can you do, when you never put yourself in a learning place? Besides, the world already has its share of risk takers, those Evel Knievel and daredevils seemingly unafraid to try anything and everything. You've met them. They're unafraid to tackle new skills and just charge ahead into uncertain territory. The world has its share of those who will climb Mount Everest just because it is there or swim the English Channel just because it hasn't been done that way before. Some people will climb on a motorcycle and jump water fountains in Caesar's Palace just to see if they can do it. Or climb into a boxing ring with men half their age just to see in they can win. They seem fearless, and they make the hardest tasks seem simple.

Risk takers expand our horizons and the boundaries of the achievable. Thank God for the risk takers who show us that our physical, mental, and cultural limitations can be overcome at any time. Some women in every generation do not read the memos about learned ignorance and learned helplessness. In the 1800s, Alethia Browning Tanner, an en-slaved woman, purchased her own freedom, along with the freedom of seventeen of her family members and friends. Nineteenth-century re-former Elizabeth Cady Stanton stayed home to raise her seven children and wrote articles for the *New York Tribune* at the same time. A teacher by the name of Dolores Huerta got tired of seeing her students come to class hungry in Stockton, California, so she quit her job and helped or-ganize the United Farm Workers with Cesar Chavez, becoming its first vice president. The women in Myra Bradwell's generation were consid-ered too dainty, needing to be protected by men. That is what the Supreme Court ruled in 1873 when it upheld *Bradwell* vs. *Illinois*, and barred women from being lawyers. Bradwell had graduated from law school, passed the bar in the state of Illinois, and edited a legal journal, but was denied admission to the bar.

Maria Mitchell grew up and became a librarian, an acceptable ca-reer for a woman in the early 1800s. Growing up on Nantucket island, she developed a love of watching the heavens with her father, and in the evenings she moonlighted by working with her father. Mitchell discov-ered a new comet in 1847, and later became the first woman elected to the American Academy of Arts & Sciences in Boston. Sojourner Truth was not acquainted with learned helplessness:

> *"Dat man ober dar say dat womin needs to be helped into car-riages, and lifted ober ditches, and to hab de best place everywhar. Nobody eber helps me into carriages, or ober mud-puddles, or gibs me any best place!" And raising herself to her full height, and her voice to a pitch like rolling thunder, she asked. "And ain't I a woman? Look at me! Look at my arm! (and she bared her right arm to the shoulder, showing her tremendous muscular power). I have ploughed, and planted, and gathered into barns, and no man could head me! And ain't I a woman? I could work as much and eat as much as a man—when I could get it—and bear de lash as well! And ain't I a woman? I have borne thirteen chilern, and seen*

'em mos' all sold off to slavery, and when I cried out with my
mother's grief, none but Jesus heard me! And ain't I a woman?"

(ELIZABETH CADY STANTON, SUSAN B. ANTHONY,
AND MATILDA JOSLYN GAGE EDS.
HISTORY OF WOMAN SUFFRAGE, 2ND. ED. VOL. 1.
ROCHESTER, NY: CHARLES MANN, 1889).

More than a hundred years ago, a butter-and-egg woman was trying to help her husband raise ten children. Her husband, John H. Murphy, Sr., had a dream of owning his own business. His children would always have jobs, and people would address him with respect. Martha, his wife, didn't read the learned helplessness memo and she saved two hundred dollars of her butter-and-egg money. When the opportunity came to purchase printing equipment from a failed enterprise, she gave it to her husband to start the Afro-American Newspaper Company. It grew to become one of the largest chains of black weekly newspapers in the country.

We admire risk takers' strength, tenacity, courage, and willingness to run ahead into uncharted territory. We admire them, love them, and hate them all at the same time. Often these risk takers are not appreciated. They are valued, but are misunderstood, considered foolish and often called impractical. We hate them because as soon as we get used to something they come along and tell us there is something else up ahead. As soon as we get comfortable, these risk takers come along and unsettle us, set another goal for us, or show us we have still more to learn.

The Bible has its share of risk takers. While others stood around all day, David took the risk and went out to challenge Goliath. Abraham took the risk and left home when everybody else wanted to stay behind. Do you think Esther really wanted to go see the king, when she took her own life in her hands but went to see him anyhow? While Martha was concerned about the kitchen and the house, Mary took a risk and sat at Jesus' feet to hear him teaching. While everybody else went home, Gideon took a few good men and dared to tackle the enemies of God. Moses went into the wilderness not knowing when he would arrive in the promised land but knowing that he would get there one day. It was Jesus who said to those who came to warn Herod, "Tell that old fox I'm going to do what my father called me to do; I'm going to heal, preach, and then when I get good and ready I'll lay my life down." (Luke 13:32)

The Bible shares stories of many risk takers. It also contains a special lesson in risk management. Risk takers need three things. They need prayer, the vehicle through which God lets them know all things are possible. They need the presence of God to support them to help them get things done. They need the power of God. It is a power beyond self that enables them to do what they've never done before and go where they've never gone.

Those risk takers in the Bible didn't do it all alone, they took their challenges to the Lord in prayer. Prayer changes things; the way to find motivation is through prayer. In Matthew 14 we find that only Peter got out of the boat to venture into the unchartered waters of life. The boat held twelve men, but only one spoke up and volunteered to risk the impossible, only one saw an opportunity, only one met the challenge and followed Jesus when he said "Come." Twelve men in the boat, but only one willing to step out on faith. Peter was willing to believe he could walk on water if God said it was okay. "Jesus, if you tell me to come over here, I'll do it. If you tell me to try this thing, I'll try it." Stores are full of books, magazines, videos, and training courses all marketed to motivate you to achieve. They are all intent on accentuating the positive and cleaning out the negative, priming you and pumping you full to motivate you to climb to the top. But you can read all the books and view all the videos, subscribe to all the magazines and take all the pills and potions you can find, but if you don't get down on your knees in prayer, you'll never climb up the ladder of success. Maybe if Peter had prayed a little bit more he would have been able to cross the whole sea instead of just going a few feet. Nothing works like prayer; it goes to the heart's source of power and releases that God power on your behalf. Good stuff happens when you pray. Solomon prayed and the temple was built. David prayed and armies were defeated. Moses prayed and seas parted. Daniel prayed and the lions got lockjaw. Esther prayed and the Hebrews were spared. Nehemiah prayed and the wall was built. A hundred and twenty men went into the Upper Room to pray together and suddenly there was a sound of a mighty rushing wind and flames were leaping over their heads. Good stuff happens when you pray. The Word tells us a storm came up, and the winds and waves began to distract Peter's eyes from his goal of reaching Jesus. We must understand that the enemies of our soul, God's enemies, have a job to do and that is to distract you and disrupt you from reaching your goal.

How do we keep our eyes on Jesus? How do we reach our goals? The Lord says to never give up on what you know you should do. Focus your attention on your goals in such a way that disappointments don't shatter you. Move ahead, knowing that one day the wind is going to blow and the waves will come up. Peter's problem was that he began to pay more attention to his obstacles than he did to his goal of reaching Jesus. He took his eyes off his goal and started to focus on the wind and the waves. When you take your eyes off your target and start paying more attention to your obstacles, you will sink every time. Focus in such a way that you become impervious to your external circumstances and to the wind and waves that come your way. Things will happen, but they will not distract you because you have your eyes straight ahead. In your time of weariness or weakness, when it doesn't seem there is a light at the end of the tunnel, keep focusing on your goal. Put it in your mind that this is not where I am staying; this is where I'm going. Understand that taking a risk to do what you are called to do means that you must face your critics. God's invitation to develop a new course of action and go where you have not gone before, break the mold, and open new doors makes you a target for those who don't want you to walk on water. Some people don't like water. With risk comes ridicule and the bad rap of being a fool trying something new. But if God has called you to do it, keep trying until you get there. A dream's worst enemy is the people out there who see the dream as a threat to their own being. Be like Peter. Be a fool for God. Never give up on what the Lord has called you to do.

Jerry's wife risked missing out on a lot of life by controlling Jerry through her learned helplessness. Somewhere deep down she knew that the risk she took by controlling their relationship meant she was sacrificing a more fulfilling and satisfying life for both of them. But, she reasoned, she didn't risk the possibility of losing him if he was always on a short leash. Her short leash kept Jerry physically present, but mentally resenting her and probably pushing her away. If she really wants to grow close to Jerry, she needs to confront her past and stop controlling him. She needs to try to understand what makes her so needy, and then take responsibility for her own life—to take control of her own life, not Jerry's. Like the Samaritan woman, she needs to have a well experience.

Considering the culture in which the woman at the well lived, she took some huge risks. First, she spoke to a Jew. You just didn't do that where she came from. Second, she spoke to a man, and she was a woman with a lousy reputation who took the chance of making it worse in this moment. Once engaged in conversation, she recognized the opportunity before her to make life better. She accepted the new course of action by running back to tell those in her community, those community folk who had not treated her with kind regard. She didn't know how they would respond, and she didn't care. She knew she had to take the risk and go tell them about this man who had spoken to her even though he knew all about her issues. What she tried so hard to hide, he addressed openly. When he did, those mistakes lost their paralyzing hold over her life. "I know all about you," he told her, "and I still choose to talk to you." He even accepted her and selected her as the first person to hear his Good News. Jesus came that we may obtain abundant life. (John 10:10, KJV). The abundant life does not exempt you from bumps, scrapes, and storm-tossed seas or deep, dark, desolate valleys. It is not a carte blanche for blue skies and sunshine. It is life with the divine presence of Christ in you. The Good News of Christ's presence is that Jesus sets the table with forgiveness at each place with grace and mercy on either side of the plate. Jesus justifies, and the Samaritan woman heard the messianic confession first.

Life calls us to move from our comfort zones on the shore to take a chance in the middle of the sea. We are called not to live our lives in the margins of history's pages, but to participate in history as it happens. If we only dared to take the risk to live life to its fullest! Sometimes we are called to use skills we're not sure we really have. Life calls us to go out where we have no one, where we have nothing we can trust except God, who called us there in the first place. We are called to live center stage, equipped only with the skills we have, equipped with the knowledge that if we just take one step God will help us to take two. Believing may mean going where you have never been, trying what you have never done, seeing what others cannot see, lifting those things that others have been unable to lift, opening doors that have been closed for generations, uncovering formulas that have remained elusive until now. Life calls us to stand, and yet we sit. Life calls us to move ahead, and yet we stand around wondering if we should take the first step. Life calls us to act, and we stand here dialoging day after day, rehearsing, researching, and wondering if others will support what we do. Life is not a dress rehearsal.

Think of Peter getting out of the boat. Christ called many to come, but Peter acted. He had his doubts, but Christ was there for him. Get out of whatever boat is holding you back from walking out on water. Get out of the boat of self-centeredness. Get out of the boat of selfishness. Get out of the boat of gossip spreading, maligning, mud slinging, and backstabbing. Get out of the boat of fear, unconfessed sin, derogatory attitudes, and conceitedness. Get out of the boat and rock the world, stir up the stew because there is too much turkey on the top and too much beef on the bottom. Create new pathways, establish new agendas, and pioneer new parts. The twenty-first century is waiting for your special gifts, and you don't have time to wait; you need to get going right now. Bring some fresh energy to some old problems. Come on and get a new approach to some age-old hangups. Set a new pattern, take the lead, speak up, stand up, get out, and change the world with Jesus. Take a chance and pray, praise God, throw your hands back and do not be ashamed of the

Gospel of Jesus Christ. We're not living a life of faith with our backs against the wall. We're in it to go all the way.

CHALLENGE TO CHANGE

Jesus strikes up a conversation with an anonymous woman coming to the well at the wrong hour of the day with her one hope. He speaks to her in such a way that demands a response from a woman taught by her culture to be silent and secluded. Jesus said to the Samaritan woman, "If you knew . . ." Ignorance is not bliss. Part of changing involves taking risks, but part of changing involves seeking knowledge, using it, and acting on it. If you knew more than you know now, how different would your life be? If you knew that the marriage was going to fail years later, would you have gotten married? If you knew the man wouldn't marry you, would you have had his baby? If you knew you could win, would you have played the game? If you knew the trouble your actions would cause, would you have behaved in an ungodly way? If you knew they would hire someone else, would you have applied for the job? If you knew the test was benign and the prognosis positive, would you have gone to the doctor sooner? If you knew things were going to work out, would you have accepted the challenge? If you knew Jesus was going to be at the well, would you have gone with the Samaritan woman? If you knew Jesus was stopping by the Pool of Bethesda, would you have gone? If you knew Jesus was going to eat dinner at Zaccheus's house, would you have stopped to eat? If you knew Jesus was going to feed five thousand, would you have stayed for the teaching? If you knew he was going to cleanse the lepers, would you have brought him your sickness and diseases? If you knew he could raise the dead, straighten a woman's crooked back, and dry up another woman's menses, would you have reached down to touch the hem of his garment? If you had known more up-front, would you have changed your behavior or made another decision?

It's like the story about an elderly man with a few friends who lived alone in a high-rise apartment building. Only a few people paid attention to the old man, spoke to him in the hall, or stopped in to see him on rare occasions. One or two of his neighbors sometimes invited the old man to share their family holiday dinner meal. Time took its toll on the old man and he grew weak and died. He left instructions with an attorney that he wanted his funeral service held at four A.M. The attorney called all of his neighbors and his few friends to invite them to the funeral service. Only two appeared. One was an elderly man who lived next door, and the other was a single mother who brought him Sunday dinner every week from her church. After the funeral home minister had preached the eulogy, the lawyer read the details of the old man's will. He had left a million dollars to be divided by those who attended his funeral service. The two who made the effort to attend each walked out with five hundred thousand dollars. When the other neighbors and the dead man's few friends heard what happened, they were stunned. They had no idea that the old man had that much money. They were upset and felt stupid that they had ignored the invitation. You can imagine what they were saying: "If I had only known then what I know now, things would be different. I would be rich!" The invitation was extended. But for various reasons—apathy, insensitivity, inconvenience, or preoccupation with their own lives—they refused the invitation. They remained ignorant and broke. Ignorance is not bliss, and it is often expensive. Jesus said to the Samaritan woman, if you knew what I had and who I was, your behavior would be different. You would be asking me for water. The woman of Samaria took a risk when she went to the well, and she took a risk to go back to the city and tell everyone what had happened. She took that risk, and her life was changed.

CALL TO ACTION

Is there something knocking at the door of your heart? Do you need to find healing over past hurts? Are you aware of areas of learned ignorance in your life? Be aware of the knowledge you have and the knowledge you need to get. Then do something about it! What are you going to do with the rest of your life? The challenge of making your life change is taking a risk. Jesus said to the Samaritan woman, if you had the knowledge, you would be asking me for living water. The best place to find motivation is in prayer. Are there things you need to know and are avoiding learning? Jesus proved His love for you by sacrificing His very best gift so that you would have the power to live today and the promise to live with Him forever in eternal life. How can you turn down a God like this for death? Take a risk and allow the promises of God to become fully yours for the first time in your life. Take a chance; you will not be disappointed. Accept the challenge to change!

Discipline of the Well

Well Lesson

The first lesson from the well is that you are capable and on your way to changing professions, from midwife to birth mother. You can do it! Being the one who helps deliver potential is a noble profession, and not to be taken lightly. Giving birth to new ideas, potential, and possibilities is miraculous. Giving birth to your own new realities through Jesus Christ is a goal of personal transformation. As you are bombarded with temptations of ignorance and helplessness daily, remember that they have the power to enslave you. Don't allow yourself to speak the language of ignorance and helplessness. Be encouraged as God grants you opportunity, and encourage others,

The second Well Lesson is that in order to change you must take some risks. Raise the standard by going beyond your comfort zone into new territory. The woman of Samaria took a risk when she went to the well, and she took another risk when she went back to the city to tell everyone what had happened. Taking risks is the enemy of learned ignorance; it builds courage and results in action. Action is what will get you beyond the current circumstances you find yourself holding on to. Action will make all the difference. Go for it—take action!

The third lesson from the well is that accepting the challenge to change is up to you. You must be the one to give yourself permission and the one to take the action. No one else can do it for you. No one else can give you the permission that you need to change. The challenge to change demands a direct response from you.

Well Words

I can do everything through him who gives me strength.

PHILIPPIANS 4:13

Every prudent man acts out of knowledge, but a fool exposes his folly.

PROVERBS 13:16

The sluggard craves and gets nothing, but the desires of the diligent are fully satisfied.

PROVERBS 13:4

. . . being confident of this, that he who began a good work in you will carry it on to completion until the day of Christ Jesus.

PHILIPPIANS 1:6

"Now to him who is able to do immeasurably more than all we ask or imagine, . . ."

EPHESIANS 3:20

Trust in the Lord with all your heart and lean not on your own un-derstanding.

PROVERBS 3:5-6

. . . we are more than conquerors . . .

ROMANS 8:37

Well Sabbatical

⁓ This is an excellent time to begin morning sabbaticals if you haven't already done so. Rise at least thirty minutes to an hour before your usual time. Go to your place of refuge and be still before the Lord. In the early morning silence, before dawn and before daily routines, ask God to show you areas of planned ignorance and planned helplessness. Make a list and see if you can trace it to a time in your childhood where it began, or write about how it has been developed and rein-forced by home, loved ones, and your own wants and desires.

⁓ Confess and repent.

⁓ Spend several mornings asking God to show you an opportu-nity to expand your world.

⁓ Look for ways to apply new information. It's possible to see things that everyone sees in a different light during prayer.

Well Language

Write these words on your file cards in a color you simply adore. Place the file cards on your mirror in the bathroom, above your light switches, on the computer-screen saver, bulletin boards, refrigerator doors, or any place you will walk by and see them on a regular basis. Write one word on several cards. Each time you see the card, repeat the word as a prayer for yourself and for others.

- ⟿ *Confident*
- ⟿ *Capable*
- ⟿ *Courageous*
- ⟿ *Consistent*
- ⟿ *Creative*
- ⟿ *Committed*
- ⟿ *You'll never know until you try.*
- ⟿ *You are equipped for the task.*
- ⟿ *Change is an opportunity to be explored, not feared.*
- ⟿ *I will commit my way to the Lord and the Divine Savior will bring it to pass.*
- ⟿ *Encouragement affirms risk.*

Well Work

1. *To do lists have been the tools of time managers for years. Your well to do list should consist of those things you do not know and need to know in your spiritual, family, work, and community life. After you have assembled your list, prioritize it. Our learned ignorance and helplessness can hold us back on our jobs and in our relationships. What do you need to know right now? What do you need to start doing yourself, right now? What do you need to learn and act upon right now?*

2. *Make a list of at least one thing you will learn or start doing in the next seven days. Do something this week for yourself that you usually put off on others because you felt you were helpless. Take a course to enhance your career, or a parenting workshop to enhance your parenting skills, or seek out a counselor for yourself or family members. There are other things you may*

need to learn, such as cutting the grass and the hedges, how to say no or how to speak up, write a report, be still and know God, or how to pray or fast.

3. *Write in your journal. Are you aware of areas of learned helplessness and ignorance in your life?*

7

A Woman Discovers a New Way of Thinking

~~~~~~~

*". . . Sir, give me this water so that I won't get thirsty and
have to keep coming here to draw water."*

JOHN 4:15

*A*urelia spent the first twenty-five years of her working life trying
to figure out what she wanted to do with the life she'd been given.
She had tried various careers, a new one every three or four years it
seemed. She said she was trying to find her space in an overcrowded environment, her place in the world, but she said it was more than just trying to find herself. In our Circle of Love one night, Aurelia told us that
she was about to resign from another job to go back to school *again* to
try something else. One of the other women in the circle listened to Aurelia's story intently and made a suggestion: "Instead of trying to figure
out what you want to do, why don't you ask the Lord what he wants you
to do?" Others joined in and encouraged her: "Instead of working on your
ideas," they pointed out, "why not work out God's ideas for your life?
God does have plans for you, plans not to harm you, but to prosper you
and give you hope and a future" (Jeremiah 29:11).

The thought had never crossed Aurelia's mind. She'd been so intent on trying to figure out her life that she never let God into the discussion of life choices, chances, and careers. Aurelia began allowing the Lord to be her career counselor. She began to pray, "Open the doors you want me to go through and close the doors on things you want me to forget. Give me the strength to walk through your open doors and not mourn the loss of shut pathways. Help me to accept your final answer."

Through the Circle of Love, Aurelia discovered she could be more. Through Jesus at the well, the Samaritan woman discovered she could be more too. As she walked to the well that hot day, she had a pretty definite idea she was—not much. But then a man spoke to her, a Jew, telling her of Living Water. This was all new and very exciting. She was introduced to a new way of thinking, as she began to heal from old wounds, she took these thoughts and dared to believe that she could be more than she had been.

Latchkey kids are youngsters left alone to fend for themselves because parents cannot be home when they get out of school. Everyone has someone to go home to but them. They wear a key, a latchkey, around their necks to school. Everyone knows that they will be on their own without supervision by adults. A latchkey personality is one that lives like there is no one to go home to. They wear their sense of abandonment for everyone to see.

Have you ever wondered if you can be more than you are? Although our heads are filled with how others and society seek to define us, if we listen we will hear the thoughts God has given us, and our true natures will be revealed. Are you listening? If you are, a new level of thinking is waiting for you.

In this chapter we'll see how visual learning through Living Water allows us to define ourselves in a whole new way according to the Creator's Divine plan; through the process of transformation a new level of thinking can ignite healing and change habits through personal investment and prayer.

DEFINING SELF

Can you be more than you are right now? It is a question that deserves serious thought. Questions compel us to move beyond our comfort zones to explore answers. Questions challenge us to think, and even if we never receive answers, these questions have a way of haunting our consciousness. Have you ever wondered what more you might do with your life? Can you be more than the educator, counselor, administrator, neighbor, student, manicurist, hairdresser, barber, farmer, rancher, rich man, poor man, baker man, thief, doctor, lawyer, or Indian chief? Can you be more that the well-endowed, underfed, malnourished, well-bred, or latch-key personality you are today? Has it ever occurred to you that you can be more than you are right now? Do you think it is possible? Would it stretch the limits of your imagination? Is it recorded within the realm of reality that you can be more than you are right now? You can be more than a sum total of genes and chromosomes surrounded by a molecular structure, more than the frame that surrounds you, which is both fragile and flexible. You can be more than hundreds of miles of vascular tubing, more than an assemblage of electrical impulses, calcium deposits, and gray matter, more than flesh and blood, uniquely fashioned into a protective epidermal covering.

Even in our society, which condones exclusionary philosophies and governmental policies, you can dare to be more. Our society promulgates voluntary enslavement to isms such as racism, sexism, classism, and any other ism that constructs glass ceilings, concentration camps, ghettos, and separate but equal. You can be more, even in a society that supports the productive but casts aside the nonproductive, such as the very young, very old, sick, poor, and afflicted. You can be more than you are in a hostile system that blames its victims. Have you wondered whether you could be more than your silent and excluded sisters of antiquity? You can be more than a monologue when you engage in a dialogue with the cosmos, more than a late-night news sound bite or a generational stereotype of "buy it and be happy." You can be more than a midnight visitation, a weekend wonder, a booty call, right-hand woman, or an ace in the hole. Is it possible for you to be more than what Marian Wright Edelman calls a risk taker, team player, detail tender, moral guerilla, organizer, mobilizer, or long-distance runner? Strive to be more than a hypocrite, attention-hogger, blamer, complainer, or a fair-weather friend or lover. Has the thought ever occurred to you that you can be more than you are right now?

The insecurities of the king of Syria led him to send a great host of horses and chariots to the city where the prophet Elisha lived. When the prophet's servant looked out the window in the morning, he saw that they were surrounded. He wondered about their survival in the face of such a large army. Elisha replied, "Fear not: for they that be with us are more than they that be with them" (2 Kings 6:16). The prophet prayed. "Lord, I pray thee, open his eyes, that he may see. And the Lord opened the eyes of the young man; and he saw: and, behold the mountain was full of horses and chariots of fire round about Elisha" (2 Kings 6:17). It was the encounter of the Divine in prayer that helped the servant see what his senses could not process. "Even the Spirit of truth; whom the world cannot receive, because it seeth him not, neither knoweth him: but ye know him; for he dwelleth with you, and shall be in you" (John 14:17, KJV).

Paul writes to the fledgling Corinthian congregation about receiving knowledge and wisdom from the Holy Spirit. The Spirit searches all things, he says, even the deep things of God. The Spirit reveals the secret wisdom of God. Not even the ruler of that age understood it (1 Corinthians 2:6–9). "The man without the Spirit does not accept the things that come from the Spirit of God, for they are foolishness to him and he cannot understand them, because they are spiritually discerned" (1 Corinthians 2:14).

The Samaritan woman walks to the well seeking physical solace, not spiritual solace. She knows the drill. She knows what's what. She knows her deal in life. She knows what's ahead. But her knowledge of

who she is has all been based on her culture's discernment of her circumstances, not the Spirit's. That changes when Jesus engages her with
a simple question, "Will you give me a drink?" Jesus asked approximately
153 questions in the Bible, using questions in several ways: as a means to
cut off his questioners or to encourage reflection. When he was interro-
gated, Jesus asked after the parable of the Good Samaritan, "And who is
my neighbor?" (Luke 10:36). When questioned about paying taxes, Jesus
asked, "Show me a denarius. Whose portrait and inscription are on it?"
"Ceasar's," they replied. He said to them, "Then give to Caesar what is
Caesar's, and to God, what is God's" (Luke 20:24–25). Jesus also used
questions to encourage the listener to become involved. A question gave
the listener the option to reject or invest in the discussion. People could
discover the answers for themselves or explore issues at their own pace.
Jesus opens the conversation with a question, and by doing so he intro-
duces the possibility of questioning, of wanting more. Had the thought
ever crossed the Samaritan woman's mind before this meeting that she
could be more than she was at that moment? Was there more to life than
she was living? Had she considered being greater than her community's
opinion of her and more than her low self-esteem allowed? Could she
live beyond the narrow cultural definition of her femininity? Like many
of us, the Samaritan woman needed a thought instigator, a thought
planter, a thought adjuster, a thought molder, a thought creator, and a
thought guide. She needed a thought provoker of the Divine kind.

A DIFFERENT HARVEST REQUIRES
A DIFFERENT SEED

Nothing in life really changes without a personal investment, personal
reflection, and personal transformation. We are concerned about the
transformation of society, culture, home, relationships, career, and
lifestyle without realizing that nothing transpires without personal investment and reflection. In order to think in a new way, a new level of

thinking is necessary. A different harvest requires a different seed. We need to think beyond the customary: "We have always done it this way." To think beyond tradition: "It was good enough for mother, it was good enough for father, and it's good enough for me." To think beyond learned ignorance and learned helplessness: I can't do that. To think beyond tunnel vision: the me, myself, and I that reign in the community must be expanded to the "whosoever will" of the sanctuary.

The thoughts that are structured and shaped by our five senses: taste, touch, sight, hearing, and smell can be captured and brought into the obedience of Christ (2 Corinthians 10:5). A new level of thinking emerges not from the flesh, but is born of Christ or the Spirit of God. This is thinking with the mind of Christ, thinking thoughts that are in harmony with the Word of God. Thinking as the Christ does: ". . . whatever is true, whatever is noble, whatever is right, whatever is pure, whatever is lovely, whatever is admirable—if anything is excellent or praiseworthy—think about such things" (Philippians 4:8). It is God who searches and knows our thoughts, even our anxious thoughts (Psalm 139:23). It is God who perceives our thoughts even from a distance (Psalm 139:2). That is why it is important to keep our thoughts in harmony with the Word of God, and if something terrible happens to us that lingers and harms our thoughts, we must help our minds heal with God's Word and love. Our minds are like a computer; what comes out depends upon what you, the data entry technician, put in. If you put junk in, junk will come out. If you put bitterness and hatred in, then bitterness and hatred will come out. If you put in the Word of God, the power of God will come out. If you put truth in, the truth shall set you free (John 8:32). You can push the delete button, but somewhere in the internal recesses of the machine the imprint is still there; you may not see it on your monitor, but it is there and an expert can retrieve it from your memory. The same is true for your human mental computer; you must be careful about what you expose your mind to. You can try to expunge material by pushing your mental delete button, but deep in the recesses of your gray matter, it still exists. It may be retrieved during nocturnal tossing and turning. It may rise, triggered by great highs and lows on the roller coaster of life. It may flash on our monitor at unsuspecting moments, influencing our conscious thoughts. Or it may lurk in our unconscious, acting as a silent instigator to our thoughts, words, and deeds. Ask the men and women who are rescue workers if they have been able to delete the tragic scenes of an accident from their minds. Ask the soldier returning from conflict if he or she has been able to delete the smell of death from his consciousness. Ask the survivors of the concentration camps of World War II if they have been able to delete the atrocities from their thoughts. Ask the mother who has held a dying child in her arms if those scenes have been deleted. Ask those who have looked into the face of a loved one who overdosed on drugs, or died of AIDS on the living room sofa. Ask the man who was stopped by the police on a dark highway (because "he was driving a car he should not been able to afford"), and was thrown to the ground, handcuffed, and searched if he has deleted the experience. Ask the child surfing the Internet who accidentally enters a pornographic chat room if she has erased these images from her mind. It may no longer be on their monitors, but the imprints are still lodged into their memory banks. Ask a policeman or fireman who survived the tragedy at the World Trade Center if they have been able to obliterate the sights, sounds, and smells of September 11, 2001.

Thoughts are powerful. They can drag us under if we let them, but they can empower us if we use them correctly. Thoughts are preludes to action. It's a think it, then do it, scenario. We think about going before we go. We think about the project before we begin it. We think about going to church before we go. We think about confronting our challenges before we do. We still need to think a little more before we say some things. When we continue thinking in the same old way, we can't expect to achieve different results or produce different behavior. If you want a different harvest, you must plant a different seed. Orange seeds produce oranges. Celery seeds produce celery. Potato eyes produce potatoes. Tulip bulbs produce tulips. Why keep planting oranges when it's apples you really need?

After twenty-five years, Aurelia had discovered a new way of thinking that was leading her life in a direction she had never imagined. Like the woman of Samaria, she discovered she could be more. She knew that there was more to life; she just didn't realize that God already had a plan all worked up for her. She didn't need to be frantically rushing around trying to figure it out. All she needed to do was ask God, trust, and wait upon the Lord and she would wind up with a Divine position in life. A different harvest requires a different seed. This time, Aurelia had planted the best possible seed available.

One set of thoughts puts new wine into new wine skins. New wine needs room to expand, just as new thoughts do. "No one sews a patch of unshrunk cloth on an old garment, for the patch will pull away from the garment, making the tear worse. Neither do men pour new wine into old wineskins. If they do, the skins will burst, the wine will run out and the wineskins will be ruined. No, they pour new wine into new wineskins, and both are preserved" (Matthew 9:16–17).

The Samaritan woman's conversation with Jesus began with the familiar: water. She understood water, the drawing and the hauling of it, and its importance. She was not an exegete of the Torah, not a religious leader, not an expert in the law of the prophets; she may not have listened to the great orators, philosophers, and religious persons of her time. All she knew was water. Jesus met her where she was and began with water. He didn't ask her to teach Sunday school, come to Bible study, pray for others, usher, or sing in the choir. All Jesus asked her for was water. In an area where water is in such short supply it is not surprising that it figures prominently in communal life. Biblically, in Psalms 23:2 or in Isaiah 32:2, water is a symbol of spiritual refreshment and God's blessing. In Ezekiel's vision the waters poured out from under the threshold as a symbol for God's unrestricted flow of blessings. In Jeremiah God is described as a fountain of living waters (Jeremiah 2:13, 17:13). Jesus presents Living Water as eternal life; the supreme blessing God gives is not just physical nourishment, but spiritual refreshment as well (John 4:14). Jesus asks the Samaritan woman for water. He starts the conversation with a discussion of a physical need, but as we see here, these physical needs often remind us of our spiritual needs. Just before John relates the Samaritan woman's story, he tells the story of another meeting that underscores how Jesus talks about the body and the Spirit, the physical and the spiritual.

In chapter three, John records a dialogue between a religious leader, Nicodemus, and Jesus. The Pharisee came to Jesus in the middle of the night, an unusual hour for instruction, much the same way the Samaritan woman came to the well at an unusual hour for drawing water. Nicodemus did not want to be seen. The Samaritan woman did not want to be seen by her community either. In the ensuing dialogue, the theological message of being born again was shared. "I tell you the truth, no one can see the kingdom of God unless he is born again," (John 3:3). Nicodemus misunderstood; he thought of the new birth as being physically born again from the womb. Jesus was speaking on a spiritual level, being born of the spirit and not of the flesh. Nicodemus was thinking concretely, physically, and Jesus was speaking abstractly and spiritually. The Samaritan woman was responding to Jesus on the physical level, and Jesus was leading her to the spiritual.

The conversation starts with the physical, but Jesus moves to the spiritual. The woman understands water. That's why she is there. Jesus increases her stake in the conversation by creating a desire in her for this special Living Water. This is an exercise in visual learning. Jesus uses water as a visual aid to paint a word image into the Samaritan woman's mind. Water evokes familiar experiences, engages the imagination, feelings and emotions rush in, and she begins to probe, to seek, to question herself. In other Bible stories Jesus uses salt and light to describe disciples. He uses a mustard seed to talk about faith, and a pearl to explore the complex theological subject of the Kingdom of God. Here, Jesus prompts the Samaritan woman into life-changing patterns of behavior by engaging her mind. He moves from the concrete to the abstract. "How can you get this living water?" she replies. She must have been thinking, "You have no ropes. You have no rocks. You didn't bring any water pots.

There are no other tools present by which you can get this living water." She questions the questioner, "Are you greater than the Jacob who gave us this well?" We, on this side of the Resurrection, understand that yes, Jesus is greater than the Jacob who gave the well in the first place. Jesus leads the idea further by saying, "Everyone who drinks this water will be thirsty again, but whoever drinks the water I give him will never thirst. Indeed, the water I give him will become in him a spring of water welling up to eternal life" (John 4:13–14).

The process of transformation has already begun. Jesus draws her into an unexpected conversation, a conversation where a question causes her to invest herself into the discussion. She responds with a request for the Living Water he speaks about. The Samaritan woman is now invited to leave the physical understanding of water and enter a new spiritual level of continuous spiritual refreshment. But like many of us who hear the message, but haven't yet understood it, the Samaritan woman continues to think of her physical needs. She feels she now has the answer to all her problems. She hears on the physical level that if she gets this Living Water, then everything will be all right in her life. "If I have Living Water, I won't have to walk out here every day in the heat and dust to get water. If I have Living Water I will never have to replenish the supply. I will never have to stand in the scorching sun, and if I have Living Water, I don't have to suffer from the stares of the townspeople; I can remain out of sight and out of mind. I can do what I want and when I want with all the spare time Living Water creates for me. If I have Living Water, my problems will be solved, and I won't have to put up with the tongue lashing of my neighbors and my friends. If I have Living Water, it will save me time and energy. With Living Water, folks won't bother me any more. Yes, give me this Living Water, and I won't have to come to this well again."

Jesus uses a question to draw the woman into a dialogue that instigates personal involvement. He initiates the transformation process with a conversation, and within the dialogue lies a basic theological message. "Do not conform any longer to the pattern of this world, but be transformed by the renewing of your mind" (Romans 12:2). The woman thought that a temporary physical solution was the answer to her problems. Water is a necessary part of life. She knew that this water would somehow solve her problems, but not how. She misdiagnosed her condition and her cure the same way some of us try to solve our problems by external gratification. If we satisfy our physiological needs, then we think everything will be all right. If we buy enough, save enough, work enough, drink enough, exercise enough, then everything will be okay. If that were a true thought then the rich, the famous, the powerful, the strong, and the high and mighty would never find clouds darkening their lives. Possessions and physical satiation do not guarantee success, satisfaction, or security. Wealth is not a guarantor of health. Wealth can secure health care, but it cannot provide healing. Too many people born with little have lived more satisfying and successful lives than those to the manor born. Too many people who have everything physical and nothing spiritual are living unsatisfied, unsuccessful lives.

The Samaritan woman thought that water would solve her problems, when what she needed to discover was the healing power of Jesus. She thought that satisfying her physical needs would solve all her problems. It's just like some of us think we can eat our way out of our problems. Some try to escape their problems through alcohol and drugs. Some think sex cures relationship problems like it satisfies their biological urges. Some believe that external, physiological, and biological stimulus can relieve our stress, our loneliness, our hurt, our pain, our anger, and our depression. But when we suffer, physical solutions can only offer limited help. The physical is the conduit to the spiritual. Jesus leads the Samaritan woman from the physical understanding of water to the spiritual understanding of Living Water as eternal life. Life is more than what our eyes see, our ears hear, our mouths taste, and our hands touch. The journey to the spiritual is through the physical, though physical solutions are inadequate to solve spiritual problems. Yet we insist on only experiencing life through these senses. Living Water defies reason, confuses scientific data, refutes proven theories, opposes our value and belief systems; our senses fail to comprehend it. You can hear, taste, touch, see, and feel water. But Living Water, how do I draw it? No one has ever seen God and still we use very physical anthropomorphic terms to describe God who is Spirit. We speak of the right hand of God, the voice of God, and the backside of God, or being safe in the arms of God. The physical is used to describe the spiritual.

The Holy Spirit is the bridge between the concrete and the abstract, the bread and the Bread of Heaven, the light and the Light of the World, the water and the Living Water. Jesus engages the Samaritan woman by speaking of water. He appeals to something familiar in her life, and creates a desire for change, a desire for what he is offering on the spiritual level. The process of transformation, the gift of Living Water, is ours for the asking. Thoughts are preludes to action. When we become conscious of our thoughts and how they provoke behavior, new ways of thinking become possible that allow us to achieve new results. After twenty-five years of floundering Aurelia finally got some sound advice from another woman in the Circle of Love. She decided to try something new and different. She decided to be open to God. She moved beyond her learned ignorance and brought her one hope to the One whose hand guides all kairos moments. She adopted a whole new way of thinking. Nothing changes without personal investment, and personal reflection.

The Samaritan woman began that day to see water in a new way. There was something more to the water that Jesus was offering. The Samaritan woman did not know about it, nor did she fully understand it. Yet she reached for it anyhow. It takes faith to reach beyond what your eyes can see, ears can hear, and hands can touch. The Samaritan woman was encouraged to move to a new level of thinking. It was a level of thinking that was spiritual, but stimulated by physical images to help her grasp the theological implications. Jesus expertly drew the images, and she reached for what he offered. The human spirit is often described as the self. You have a physical heart, a marvelous muscle that pumps blood throughout your body. You can live without tonsils, appendix, an ovary and a uterus, but you cannot live without a physical heart. You also have a spiritual heart. Invisible to you, this heart is the seat of lust and meditation, desire and doubt, pride, purpose, reason, thought, obedience, and rebellion. It is this heart that Jesus gives to men when it is broken (Isaiah 61:1–3). God can give us a clean heart to follow him. A new heart circumcised that can respond to the spiritual.

CALL TO ACTION

Thoughts are preludes to action. When we become conscious of our thoughts and how they influence behavior, new ways of thinking become possible that allow us to achieve new results. Become conscious of your thoughts and how they provoke your behavior. Where do those thoughts come from? Does the past or the present prompt them? In prayer, ask God to capture every thought and bring all your thoughts in obedience to Christ (2 Corinthians 10:5). Positive thoughts going into the mind leads to positive thoughts coming out of the mind. If the thought is dangerous, disruptive, or destructive ask God to replace it with whatever is pure, true, praiseworthy, and excellent (Philippians 4:8). If the thoughts lead you down the same old road, to do the same old thing, and in the same old undesirable direction ask the Instigator of Thought to renew your mind with a new level of thinking. Begin where you are by asking Jesus for Living Water, and the Spirit of Truth will lead you toward transformation. Praise God for seeing you through the past and giving you a new level of thinking in Christ Jesus.

Discipline of the Well

Well Lesson

The first Well Lesson is that whatever positive or negative thoughts go into the mind come out in our lives. When positive thoughts come to our minds we must take the utmost care in feeding and nurturing them. The knowledge of the Spirit reveals the wisdom of God. It is the Spirit that allows us to search the deep things of God. Let the Spirit of God fill your mind with what is true and right and good. You'll be glad you did!

The second Well Lesson in discovering a new way of thinking is that just because you cannot see it or explain it does not mean it is not real. It's hard for us sometimes to understand the nonmaterial aspects of life. You have a soul and you cannot see it. You cannot see, taste, touch, or feel it, yet you have a spirit. When was the last time you saw a microwave, an X ray, an FM radio wave or an electrical impulse as it raced across your brain when thoughts arose? Trust in the Lord with all your heart and lean not on your own understanding.

The third Well Lesson is to know that physical solutions are inadequate to solve spiritual problems. Physical solutions may provide temporary escape or comfort, but they are just Band-Aids and not a cure. They are not the silver bullets or magic pills to end all your problems. Jesus just gave the Samaritan woman the tip of the spiritual iceberg; she could not have handled much more. It's much like when Jesus was teaching the disciples about the work of the Holy Spirit and said, "I have much more to say to you, more than you can now bear" (John 16:12). She came for water, but needed a relationship with God through Jesus

Christ, much like the beggar begging alms at the Gate Beautiful when Peter and John went to the temple to pray in the days following the death and resurrection of Jesus. The man wanted alms. Peter said that the silver and gold the man wanted, he did not have. But he did have what the man needed. "In the name of Jesus Christ of Nazareth, walk" (Acts 3:6). The woman came for water, and Jesus had exactly what she needed. She needed what no human being could give her: dignity, integrity, forgiveness, redemption, acceptance, belonging, being, and doing. Jesus could give her living water, the eternal spiritual refreshment.

Well Words

. . . If there is a natural body, there is also a spiritual body.

1 CORINTHIANS 15:44

The spiritual did not come first, but the natural, and after that the spiritual.

1 CORINTHIANS 15:46

So we fix our eyes not on what is seen, but on what is unseen. For what is seen is temporary, but what is unseen is eternal.

2 CORINTHIANS 4:18

Since we live by the Spirit, let us keep in step with the Spirit.

GALATIANS 5:25

Now the Lord is the Spirit, and where the Spirit of the Lord is, there is freedom.

2 CORINTHIANS 3:17

Do not conform any longer to the pattern of this world, but be transformed by the renewing of your mind.

ROMANS 12:2

. . . we take captive every thought to make it obedient to Christ.

2 CORINTHIANS 10:5

> *... whatever is true, whatever is noble, whatever is right, whatever is pure, whatever is lovely, whatever is admirable—if anything is excellent and praiseworthy—think about such things.*

PHILIPPIANS 4:8

Well Sabbatical

⌒ As you continue taking your daily planned rest periods, fill your mind with the Word of God. Reflect on the things Paul suggests in Philippians 4:8, and bring every thought under the control of Christ (2 Corinthians 10:5).

⌒ Read Romans 8:1–11. Pray that the Holy Spirit will be your teacher and guide to understanding God's Word. Pray and ask God to help you to become a spiritual woman so that you can discern spiritual things. Without the Spirit things that come from the Spirit of God are foolishness (1 Corinthians 2:14–16).

⌒ Be still and know God. Allow the Lord to guide you from physical meanderings to the things of the Spirit. Daniel prayed for understanding. The answer to his prayer was delayed for twenty-one days. It was not a physical obstruction, but a disruption in the spiritual (Daniel 10:12–14). As the disciple Stephen was being stoned by a hostile mob, he looked from his earthly physical crisis to see into the spiritual. He looked and saw Jesus standing in heaven at the right hand of the Father (Acts 7).

Well Language

⌒ A different harvest requires a different seed.
⌒ Think new ways to achieve new results.

⟶ Think on what is true, pure, lovely, excellent, holy, right, noble and praiseworthy.

⟶ I shall be transformed by the renewing of my mind.

⟶ Thoughts precede action.

⟶ Godly thinking produces Godly action.

⟶ Let's get spiritual.

Well Work

1. Spend time reading through the Gospels to discover the questions Jesus asked during his three-year earthly ministry. Here is a sampling of questions to get you started:

    ⟶ "Do you believe I am able to do this?" Matthew 9:28

    ⟶ "To what can I compare this generation?" Matthew 11:16

    ⟶ "And why do you break the command of God for the sake of your tradition?" Matthew 15:3

    ⟶ "Who do the people say the Son of Man is?" Matthew 16:13

    ⟶ "What do you want me to do for you?" Luke 18:41

    ⟶ "Do you believe in the Son of Man?" John 9:35

    ⟶ "What is the Kingdom of God like? What shall I compare it to?" Luke 13:18

2. Read the questions and let them inspire you to a new level of thinking as you study the Gospels. Begin to discover new realities as you are prompted to become a participant in the spiritual. Remember to ask the Holy Spirit to be your teacher and guide through God's Word.

3. Write in your journal the answer to: Can you be more than you are now?

8

A Woman Faces Her Past

"Go, call your husband and come back."

JOHN 4:16

*J*enessa looked back and all she saw were too many hours left home alone with Uncle Ted while Mom went to work. He always wanted to play his favorite game, doctor. He examined her body and gave her unwanted gynecological exams. He threatened to hurt her and her mother if she ever told anyone: Who would believe her anyway? In the presence of Christ, Jenessa was able to go from victim to victor. She was able to face her past and realize that being abused was not her fault—she was a child—and most men are not like Uncle Ted, who was sick and evil.

Healing past wounds is a significant step in the process of personal transformation. The past is like dust collecting in the living rooms of our lives. We rarely want to disturb the dust as it lies like an almost invisible film on everything. The past is too traumatic, too painful, or too troublesome to deal with. Sometimes the dust of the past becomes so thick, it must be cleaned away with specialized cleaners that attract the particles and erase their residue. Thick dust on your coffee table requires assistance from cleansing agents; Mr. Clean can take care of the fine dust particles around your house. Jesus can take care of the dust particles of your past, along with the residues of guilt and shame.

The Samaritan woman had a past, and she was having a difficult time overcoming it. She was down to her last things. She had only one hope left, and all she could do was carry on. When she met Jesus at the well, she learned that before she could successfully go on with a satisfying life she needed to rise above the events of her past. When she accepted the Living Water Jesus offered her at the well in Samaria, she was able to rise above her past and begin her life anew through a transforming experience with Jesus.

In this chapter we'll look at how unresolved women have confronted the past in order to move on to the future. By overcoming debilitating problems and patterns, their eyes were opened and they found belonging, acceptance, and love in Christ. Have you ever had a problem that was collecting dust? Create a new beginning and clean up your past.

OVERCOMING PROBLEMS AND PATTERNS

Have you ever had a problem that lasted a long time? A problem that was more than a momentary crisis or a fleeting disappointment? Often we're held captive by the one problem that just won't go away. The cast of characters involved in your issue may long ago have moved on, but you're still replaying the feelings from that time in your life. It seems God is speaking and moving in everybody else's situations, except yours. Everyone else's problems and issues have been resolved. Others have resolved two, three, or four problems, while you are still held captive by the one problem. Your friends, family, and significant other have each prayed about their problems or issues and their prayers have been answered. They have fasted with results, and they have testified about miracles, blessings, and deliverance; they have shouted publicly and privately over the victories won. They were still before God and came to know Him over many issues. You, on the other hand, are still mad, still broke, still upset, still laid off, still hurt, still wounded, and still sick. You are still besieged by money crises, crime crises, drug crises, AIDS crises, grief crises, job crises, men crises, home crises, kid crises, grandchild crises, communication crises, production crises, and just plain crises that have lasted a long time. Life just doesn't seem fair. God is speaking and moving in everybody else's situations, except yours. Everyone else is moving on but you. Everyone else is getting better but you. Everyone is getting paid but you. Everyone is getting married but you. Everyone else's divorce is finalized but yours. Everyone else's child support check is in but yours. Everyone else's car is out of the shop but yours. Everyone else got a cost-of-living increase but you. Pamprin worked for everyone but you. Everyone is postmenopausal but you.

When Cynthia looked back all she could see was an abusive marriage. Sandra had an arthritic problem for ten long years. Her fingers curled into a fixed position until she could not put on earrings, button a blouse, open a jar or drive her car. Andrea's problem lasted twenty-two years of her daughter's forty-year life. Her daughter was diagnosed with paranoid schizophrenia; it wasn't serious enough to have her institutionalized, but serious enough so she could not live independently. Andrea and her daughter lived the problem together for a long time. Ellen had a problem that lasted a long time, her husband's fifteen-year struggle with alcoholism. Kaylee, thirty, is still living at home. She has a job that helps with her mother's household expenses, but not enough to pay rent, a car note, or school loans. Donna is back on public assistance. Ricky has genital herpes and it won't go away. Micah's husband slaps her around in front of the children. The Crafts' daughter prostitutes after school and on weekends. Anita has been shoplifting for years just for kicks. Pastor Ron cannot convince some of the men in his congregation not to use the choir as a personal dating agency. There are those having another biopsy; a persistent cough; depression; a difficult coworker; a weight problem; large breasts; overactive libidos; temper tantrums; fears that debilitate; or worries that incapacitate.

Problems are around. They always have been. The Hebrews had a four-hundred-year-long enslavement problem in the mud pits of the ghettos of Goshen in Egypt. Israel had a continuing problem of sin that led to a seventy-year captivity problem in Babylon. Moses had an Exodus congregation that mumbled, grumbled, and complained their way through the wilderness for forty long years. He saw, but never got to, the promised land. And for a really longtime problem, think of Hannah. Everyone was having babies but her. Her unproductive womb was an embarrassment in an ancient society where a woman's value was connected to her ability to produce a male child. Her adversaries tormented her year after year (1 Samuel 1:4–8). Discuss longtime problems with the woman with the issue of blood. Her money ran out and her doctors still did not know what else to do to stop her cancerous womb from bleeding. Her problem lasted twelve long years (Luke 8:43). The invalid lay with his problem at the Pool of Bethesda until it was believed that an angel came down and troubled the water. Whoever was first into the water was healed of their diseases. The man never could get into the water first and his problem lasted thirty-eight years (John 5:1–10). If you think you have longtime problems, talk to the woman who was bent over for eighteen long years and could not stand up straight (Luke 13:11).

If you want to talk about longtime problems, talk to the Samaritan woman. She was a woman with a past. But she persevered and one day her life changed. She was asked a question and she reached for a new level of thinking. Remember that nothing changes without personal investment; she was an involved participant in the process of transformation and it was time for personal reflection. The woman was not yet ready for the Living Water, there had to be an adjustment; personal transformation could only begin after she had faced her past. Jesus commanded, "Go get your husband." It was as if Jesus responded, "Go home and get your past. It is the longtime problem that needs to be addressed first." The Samaritan woman responded eagerly, saying, "Give me the Living Water so I won't have to go through what I go through to draw water from this well every day." In order to get to the new level of thinking, she had to let go of the old thinking. She had to go back before she moved forward. Oftentimes, the moment the past is revealed and confronted, transformation becomes possible—the transformation from water to Living Water occurs.

Personal transformation begins with personal reflection. The two components of personal reflection are retrieval and retrospect. Retrieval is responding to the command to "Go back and get it!" It is the active confrontation of the past, returning to the traumatic moment, and bringing to the forefront thoughts, decisions, and events that have been buried in the dust of denial. Retrieval is a good starting place, but it is not a staying place. Retrospect, on the other hand, is the act of contemplating the past. Retrospect is surveying the thoughts, decisions, and events of your autobiography, spending the necessary time, and investing in intense examination. It is revisiting the events that influence your present actions and threaten your future well-being. Retrospect is engaging in the process of reflection and review on a deeper level, examining the past in the presence of Christ. It is important to note that personal reflection is not done in isolation, but in the presence and power of the Son of God. In the presence of Christ, the Samaritan woman was given the command to go back and get her past. Retrospect is also done in the light of the present. It is examining yesterday, not from where you were, but from where you are now. Most of all, it is conducting the review in the Sonlight of God's love.

Retrospect and retrieval are not about a stroll down memory lane, or a nostalgic glance through rose-colored glasses. Rose-colored glasses tend to frame memories with a warm, fuzzy glow. Take the glasses off and engage the elements of personal reflection in an encounter with Jesus at your own Samaritan well experience. Journey to the well and look back at the experience in the presence of Christ. Conduct your survey, reviewing personal history through the eyes of Christ, with the lenses of grace and mercy.

Jesus did not castigate the Samaritan woman for past mistakes. In this ancient culture, women were protected and provided for by men, either by their fathers or their husbands. Left on their own, some women participated in uncommitted relationships to survive. Physical gratification was exchanged for provisions: a roof, a bed to sleep in, clothes to wear, and food to eat. Some women today enter uncommitted relationships for the same things: a place to live, clothes to wear, a car to drive, food to eat, and money to spend. Some call it being a kept woman and others call it prostitution. It is still the exchange of goods and services. Whether or not the Samaritan woman was initiating the relationships, or being passed around, or hired like a glorified housekeeper, or a victim of her environment, the few verses in John's gospel give us a glimpse of a cycle of pain repeating itself. For her and us to live in a different way, we must do in a different way. To do in a different way means change. It may mean we need to change friends, jobs, habits, locations, and telephone numbers. We will keep getting the same results as long as we keep doing the same things. Many times we don't do in a different way because too many people benefit from our incapacitation. Someone is benefiting from our recycled trash, maybe even us.

There is an often-told story about a man and a woman in a married relationship. The husband became upset with his wife's behavior when all of a sudden she changed. She wasn't the same woman he had married years before. They tried everything to get back on track. They prayed together, counseled with other couples, and finally, the husband had no recourse except to take his wife to a marriage counselor. As he was giving the counselor a long litany of complaints the specialist finally stopped him and wanted to know just what the exact problem was. The husband responded that his wife thought she was a chicken. The counselor instructed him "tell her she is a woman and keep telling her that she is a woman until she starts acting like a woman." He was told that if he treated her like a woman, she would respond; if he cared for her like a woman, she would act like a woman; if he respected her like a woman and talked to her like a woman, she would rise to the occasion. If he provided encouragement, she would be more woman than he could stand. Just tell her she is a woman, not a chicken. The husband seemed disappointed in the response. He looked the counselor in the eye and said, "I would tell her she is a woman, but we need the eggs!"

Sometimes we allow debilitating situations to exist because of secondary gains. We would change, but we need the eggs. Some people in our lives depend upon us staying the same, never growing, never thinking, never getting stronger, never better, never brighter, never smarter, never going anywhere, never deepening in faith and grace. These are the personal keepers of the past who, at significant times and places, never let you forget what you did, what you said, where you were, and why it will never get better. They throw your past in your face to hurt, not to heal. They do it to keep you in place, unsaved, unhealed, and undelivered. They need the eggs. Certain habits and destructive behaviors we keep around because they protect us from the risk of doing something else. We have habits that protect us from the risk of success, responsibility, authority, and visibility because we need the eggs.

Open your eyes and see the Christ who confronts you in the wilderness at the well of remembrance. You may find a woman with a past; a woman with a history of defining moments, strengths, weaknesses, blessings, curses, tenure problems, questionable decisions, profound choices, neuroses, recycled failings, and sins. Everyone has layers of undisturbed dust behind the door we want to keep hidden and dormant. Jesus stops by the well to remind us to confront and contemplate in preparation for restoration.

BELONGING, ACCEPTANCE, AND LOVE

With the help of a good counselor, supportive friends, and through the grace of God and a lot of hard work, Jenessa was able to confront her attacker legally, and began a support-group ministry for others like herself. She was an innocent victim as a child and as an adult she chose to move beyond victimhood to victory. As she said goodbye to a painful past, she felt the healing love and acceptance of Christ.

During one of our Circle of Love sessions, entitled "One Night at the Well," the women retrieved their past and engaged in retrospect. It was a powerful moment. We filled empty glasses with water that represented all the tears we had cried over the past. The lights were turned off. In the soft glow of candlelight we slowly poured our tears into a common bowl in the center of our circle. We carried our tears one last time. We cried our tears one last moment. We released our tears to make room for tomorrow. We made a conscious decision that it was time to move on! The past was a liability that the future could no longer afford to carry.

Savoka looked back on a childhood with a seriously ill mother and without a father. Her mother was too ill to raise her daughter. In the presence of Christ, she sees the classmate who took her home one day. The classmate's father became Savoka's father as well, and introduced her to a new family. "Though my mother and father forsake me, the Lord will receive me" (Psalm 27:10).

M. Peck Scott writes in his book *The Different Drum* that if Jesus the healer teaches us anything, it is that the way to salvation lies through our vulnerabilities. Once the past is revealed, a Christ who goes to the cross for others' sins unlocks the door of salvation. In hiding her past from others, the woman at the well was also hiding from herself. The moment the past was revealed and confronted, transformation became possible.

When you retrieve and retrospect in the presence of Christ, you gain through your losses, learn invaluable lessons, and take more than you thought you could take. In the presence of Christ you can see that the invisible hand of God was moving on your behalf. What looked like roadblocks were pauses for preparation. What was a disappointment was actually a blessing in disguise. What others meant for evil, God meant for good (Genesis 50:20). Through the eyes of Christ, you see that quiet was just a delay and history does not have to repeat itself. Just because you stumbled once, doesn't mean you must stumble again. You have confessed and confronted your sins, and Jesus has already forgiven you. You must now forgive yourself. You can be forgiven, and you can forgive others.

In the postmodern mind, it appears that the Samaritan woman settled for less than the best of relationships. For whatever reasons, she settled for a series of live-in, uncommitted relationships. Perhaps biological urges may have been satisfied, but lust cost her more than she was willing to give. It cost her a decent reputation, dignity, integrity, a good name, value in the community, public acceptance, and future relationships. Could it be that she was in relationships with men who took more than they gave? Love is still a two-way street. If there is give, there is also take. If there is hoarding, there should also be sharing. If there is some selfishness, there must be selflessness. The Samaritan woman was giving herself away like a drink of water on a hot summer day. This is the woman whose name we see written on the wall of the men's room or scratched into the sides of the telephone booth. Lust may satisfy the physical needs, but in the Samaritan woman's life there was no passion, intimacy, or real love. She needed healing. All she wanted was what everyone else wants: to belong, to be accepted, and to be loved. Didn't the Samaritan woman deserve at least that?

UNRESOLVED WOMEN

The Samaritan woman had a long-term problem; history kept repeating itself. She could not live beyond her unsatisfying relationships, move to a higher level of thinking. She could not be the birth mother of her own future because there were too many unresolved issues in her past. She could never achieve her one hope, because her past kept showing up in her present-day lifestyle decisions. She was an unresolved woman.

Unresolved women are those who have too many loose ends, and those loose ends refuse to be tied. Unresolved women live in perpetual stagnation. They judge every event and person by the mistakes, disappointments, failures, and upsets of the past. The issues don't keep them from existing, but they do keep them from living an abundant life. Unresolved women are the walking wounded of the world. The past was never enough to kill them, but it did enough damage to wound them. They bleed in every relationship, the past makes them tender to the touch and easily bruised, and their scars are worn like medals of honor or badges of courage visible and available for every conversation. They are sometimes uneasy around women who have resolved their child-hood, gender, cultural heritage, economic, and relational issues and their sisters' successes are an added blow to their wounded position. Some unresolved women can even make others feel guilty about being blessed in losing weight, getting a job promotion, becoming engaged, moving into a new apartment, or some perceived advantage they have not tasted or tried themselves.

The unresolved Samaritan woman was perhaps uneasy around the resolved women in Sychar, and maybe that is why she went to a dis-tant well one half mile outside the city at the hottest hour of the day to draw water alone. Jesus was there at the well, waiting for her. "Go and get you husband," he told her. Jesus already knew the sordid details. He knew the hurt, the heartbreak, the pain of rejection, and her longing for a secure relationship. He knew her desire for intimacy, companionship, and maybe just a spark of romance. The Samaritan woman looked back and said, "I have no husband." Jesus responded, "You are right when you say you have no husband. The fact is you have had five husbands and the man you now have is not one either." Jesus gave her an opportunity to confront and contemplate the past. Confession emerged in the discover-ing period. The Samaritan woman began to see her life in a new way: an uncommitted series of monogamous relationships colored with fear, de-nial, pride, isolation, shame, guilt, embarrassment, and pain. During this confrontation she was able to say, "I am examining the past from the po-sition of today. I can no longer deny the details. I confess I have no hus-band."

The Samaritan woman's relationship roulette had lasted a long time. She was a woman with a past. She was also a woman on a path to healing and becoming whole. Jesus had broken the silence, scattering the dark secret dust of guilt and shame, dissipating it in the Sonlight of Jesus Christ. Jesus challenged her to confront her past so she could move on to her future without recrimination, guilt, or shame clogging her conscious mind, influencing decisions and opinions.

Remember Jenessa, moving forward in Christ after a childhood of abuse by her Uncle Ted. She could have hung on to the tragedy of those memories, but through Jesus' Living Water she was able to find her life's motive and purpose. She did her retrieval work and retrospect work. This work is not always easy, but it is worth the effort and the discomfort that may surface to clear the air, remove any thick old dust, and live a full life. Through Jesus, Jenessa was redeemed and went on to do incredibly important work that benefited many and glorified His name.

CALL TO ACTION

Have you ever had a problem that has lasted a long time? Remember Hannah and her longtime problem? She had a baby a year later. Remember Moses? He led Israel out of bondage in Egypt. Remember the Hebrews in the wilderness? They got to the promised land. Remember the woman with the issue of blood? Her wound dried up. The man by the Pool of Bethesda? He got up. The bent-over woman? She's standing tall now. And Jesus? He is no longer on the cross, or in the grave, but seated at the right hand of God.

Confronting past problems by identifying unproductive patterns and overcoming them is the first step to creating new beginnings. After personal reflection, including retrieval and retrospect in the presence of Christ, you are ready to move toward becoming a woman without excuses.

What are you doing to reveal and confront the problems and issues in your life? Could you be doing more?

Discipline of the Well

Well Lesson

The first lesson from the well is it is necessary to confront the past if you want to be a resolved woman. Remember, we are either coming of age or coming to terms. There has to be an adjustment, a personal investment, and personal reflection identifying the unproductive patterns and problems before you take the first step to creating new beginnings. This is more than looking at memories; it's coming to terms and accepting responsibility for your own past conduct. Turn to the well of remembrance and take the necessary action for personal transformation. Jesus will meet you at the well in all his mercy to blot out your transgressions. Purify yourself from the toxins and contaminates of the past world and find a new spirit in Christ.

The second lesson from the well is Jesus gives unconditional belonging, acceptance, and love. It's available every day of the year, in good times and in bad, in happy and in sad, and it's more than any one of us could ever have without him. The loving arms of God reach a very long way.

The third Well Lesson is that as long as we remain unresolved, history will keep repeating itself. Oftentimes, the moment the past is revealed and confronted, transformation becomes possible—the door from water to Living Water opens and we can feel belonging, acceptance, and love. As 2 Corinthians 5:17 says, ". . . if anyone is in Christ, he is a new creation, the old has gone, the new has come!" The Samaritan woman's relationship roulette didn't stop until she confronted it and had a transformational experience with Jesus at the well in Samaria. Become a resolved woman; resolve to confront the past in order to transform your future.

The fourth lesson is that forgiveness is available every day. It does not matter whether your issues are ancient, recent history, or current events, when you confess God is faithful to forgive (1 John 1:9). This is not a license to do as you please. It is the escape button on your lifestyle computer to end an unproductive program or the means to reboot your life so you can reprogram your system according to the Word and will of God.

Well Words

Shake off your dust, rise up, sit enthroned, O Jerusalem. Free yourself from the chains on your neck, O captive Daughter of Zion.

ISAIAH 52:2

Have mercy on me, O God, according to your unfailing love, according to your great compassion blot out my transgressions.

PSALM 51:1

Therefore do not worry about tomorrow, for tomorrow will worry about itself. Each day has enough trouble of its own.

MATTHEW 6:34

Since we have these promises, dear friends, let us purify ourselves from everything that contaminates body and spirit, perfecting holiness out of reverence for God.

2 CORINTHIANS 7:1

Therefore, if anyone is in Christ, he is a new creation; the old has gone, the new has come!

2 CORINTHIANS 5:17

Brothers, I do not consider myself yet to have taken hold of it. But one thing I do: Forgetting what is behind and straining toward what is ahead, . . .

PHILIPPIANS 3:13

Well Sabbatical

A planned rest period is an excellent place to begin personal reflection in the presence of Christ. Take as long as necessary to disturb the dust of denial, scratching beneath the surface of living to survey past thoughts, decisions, and actions.

⌒ *Search to see if there are any recycled behaviors and habits that inhibit or debilitate. Examine the behaviors and habits that have kept you in your personal wilderness and can strengthen you in the promised land of resolution.*

⌒ *Retrieve the past. Remember, going back is not to get back or to stay back, it is to clear the air of the dust that clouds our vision and clogs our mission. Reflect upon it through the eyes of Christ and in the Word of God. A good promise book that lists God's promises may help you see yesterday in the light of the Gospel. When you disturb the dust of sin, read Psalm 51 or 1 John 1:5–10; for a trial, Psalm 26; for vengeance, Romans 12:17–21; for depression, Psalm 16, Isaiah 61:1–4; for illness, Psalm 23, Mark 1:29–34; James 5:14–16; for disasters, Romans 8:31–39; for prejudice, Ephesians 2:11–22; for fear, Psalm 27.*

⌒ *It's good to take just as much time during your Sabbatical to remember the wonderful and marvelous experiences of yesterday. The past also includes the great, the very good, and the good. Go treasure hunting for the good, and take others with you. It is good to up-link with your friends, instead of always downloading. Gather your old high school yearbooks for a "the way we were" gathering. Laugh at the old hairstyles and fashions. Make a "good times" scrapbook. Post photos of fond memories on your mirrors and refrigerator doors. Keep the good ever before you. It is just as valuable to be acquainted with these high mountain-top experiences. They can keep you afloat in your off seasons. Strengths revisited are like medicine to the spirit. Joys recalled are like a shot in the arm. The remembrance of them helps you to go from strength to strength. Look for the good and celebrate.*

~ *If the confrontation and contemplation processes are still too hard to bear, the prayerful assistance of a pastor or counselor would be beneficial.*

~ *Write in your journal about what you need to confront in the past in the presence of Christ so you can move on.*

Well Language

~ *I am ready to move on!*
~ *Reflect and resolve.*
~ *Confront, contemplate, and create new beginnings.*
~ *Look back and lean forward.*
~ *Look for the good and celebrate!*

Well Work

This exercise is excellent to do alone or in a group of supportive co-travelers.

1. *If you're in a group, sit in a circle. Place an empty bowl in the center of the circle, either on the floor or on a table.*
2. *Each participant should hold a glass of water, representing the tears of the past, all the tears you have cried without resolution.*

The water also represents the tears of the present because of the influence of the past.

3. *In the presence of Christ and in view of God's Word, each woman now prayerfully and carefully considers personal reflection, engaging in the acts of confrontation and contemplation of past issues. Ask the Divine for the intervention of the Holy Spirit to guide women into all truth, and move them toward resolution.*

4. *Stand when ready to move beyond unresolved issues: habits that hurt, the fear that inhibits, addictive reactions, self-inflicted wounds, tragedies, deaths, regrets, rejections, childhood residue of being alone, doing too much or not enough, and sins of others upon your life. Carry the glasses to the empty bowl, one at a time. Pour out the tears slowly saying, "I am ready to move on!" Continue to repeat the phrase as all the water is poured into the bowl.*

5. *Having released her tears, each woman begins to thank God. Praise God for intentionally meeting you at the well of personal reflection. Thank God for the invitation to resolution and personal transformation. "Now to him who is able to do immeasurably more than all we ask or imagine, according to his power that is at work within us . . ." (Ephesians 3:20).*

9
A Woman Without Excuses

"What you have just said is quite true."
JOHN 4:18

Rachel always used her rocky start in life as a convenient excuse for making poor relationship decisions. As an adult child of an abusive parent, she perceived that her childhood was a good reason for her own inability to control her anger. In a candlelit room full of women, she poured her tears into a bowl declaring that she was ready to move on. She decided that her earlier life could motivate her toward positive goals rather than negative.

The Samaritan woman's life had been hard and painful. She hadn't always made good choices, and now she didn't want to face the people in her community. They looked down on her because of her bad reputation, which was due to past relationship decisions, a culture that did not support or encourage women, and a lack of friends, all excuses she used for hiding out and going to the well at the wrong time of day. Her excuses were all very good, but that day she met Jesus at the well and she saw that confronting her past instead of making excuses for it could change everything. As she began to value herself and live beyond excuses, her life became a witness that would change the community she lived in.

In this chapter we will look at how we limit ourselves when we play the victim, hang on to excuses, and don't carefully consider the choices life presents to us to move beyond limitations. God gives us choices and it's up to us to be available for an opportunity, trusting God instead of our own wills to help us exercise wise decisions. When we are open to God, we are the ones who get to decide, the choice is ours.

EXCUSES ARE DECISIONS

Excuses are those marvelous things you reach for to explain to others and yourself, your lack of productivity, performance, or commitment. They are the crutches you lean on to absolve yourself of shoddy work, absence, lateness, or the mess you have made of things. Some have favorite excuses: I'm shy. I'm adopted. I'm too thin. I married too early. I married too late. I'm not married. I had children too soon. I don't have money, not enough money, or too much money. I didn't get an education, or I'm too qualified for my position. My parents didn't love me. I didn't have a pleasant childhood. I didn't have a father, or I didn't know the one I had. I was sickly growing up, or I am sick now. I don't have transportation. I'm too heavy, not experienced, too young, too old, too dark, too light, or just too tired. Excuses are decisions. Excuses are decisions with future implications. You decide to stay out late so you get to bed late and consequently are too tired to get to work on time the next day. You decide that one activity is more important than the other so you decline an invitation or don't show up as promised. You decide that the sale is more important than the tithe, and you spend the tithe. You decide that the service at St. Mattress where Pastor Pillow preaches is better than going to church, so you stay in bed. You decide to live under your circumstances rather than above them. Every disappointment, every mistake, every rejection, even the smell of victory or defeat takes you right back to your perceived barriers to success. Often, it's not what happens to you, but how you decide to respond to the event that is most important.

For many women excuses have become internalized limitations.

Excuses have become unspoken fears, boundaries you have decided to live within. They become the context that defines how far you dare to go in life. You pull out your excuses at those critical times when you are challenged about why you have settled into stagnant waters even though you have been offered Living Water. If you forget your excuses, your personal excuse-keepers conveniently remind you why you haven't seized opportunities that have come your way, or why you haven't grown beyond your present situation. It makes you wonder what you would and could do if all your excuses suddenly disappeared like sugar in a cup of hot water. What if the convenient excuses you use to pass the blame or justify your behavior suddenly disappeared? Have you ever been in a situation where someone pulled out excuse after excuse until none was left and she became perplexed, confused, and didn't know what to do? The pattern by which she made decisions had been interrupted, and she didn't know which way to turn. Have you ever watched someone run out of excuses? Some people don't know how to live without them. Not having excuses or not being able to use excuses paralyzes them from living, and they run away.

The Samaritan woman came to the well with lots of excuses. She was there because of poor relationship decisions, trying to escape prying eyes and gossiping tongues. She was there as a victim of habit, history, and heritage. All were very good excuses for why she couldn't live beyond her mistakes, but Jesus methodically peeled away her excuses one by one. He carefully moved from a discussion of water retrieval to an intimate discussion of worship, until she had no more excuses to hide behind. Jesus penetrated the excuse shield she used to deflect accusations, removing the carefully selected reasons she used to get others to indulge her negative life habits. Jesus knew how to reach into the heart of this woman, and touch the tender cords of life within. Grace flowed through her opened heart like virtue flowed from the hem of his garment into another nameless woman who had an issue of blood. Jesus was teaching her to live life decisively. Living without excuses is living a decisive life.

LIVING BEYOND LIMITATIONS

A participant in one of the Circle of Love gatherings was challenged by a progressive illness. She was very active in her church, at work, and in the community, a welcome addition to every group. Paulette lived a full life, but she grew increasingly despondent because of limited energy and declining mobility. In prayer, we were able to identify the things she could do and enjoyed doing. The illness was no longer an excuse; it became a bridge to other opportunities.

Rachel suddenly realized that she could use her experience not as an excuse for her own behavior, but as a model of how not to behave. She saw that she was using her anger about what happened to her as a weapon against others; it was her protection. Now the energy that anger created will no longer be used against others, God, or herself. Instead, she is going to use her energy to help those who are still caught.

The Samaritan woman stood in the hot desert sun, transparent to Jesus Christ. The reasons why she came to the well at the wrong time of day were forgotten, the reason why she separated herself from community disappeared, the excuses for not living fully dissipated, and the excuse of habit and history evaporated. She was a free woman who no longer needed excuses.

Eradicating excuses is a liberating experience. The problems may remain the same, but your attitude about them changes. You perceive the same problems in a different light. Learning to come out from behind the fantasy shield is the first step in living a decisive life. Some women are just like Snow White, protected by seven charming, but oddball, guys, hoping that a "real" man will come along and rescue them from the woods. Other women live like Sleeping Beauty, believing that if they lie on their back long enough they will be rescued. Then there are the Belles (as in *Beauty and the Beast*), forced into living with someone who looks like a monster, acts like a monster, and treats them like monsters. They dream it will be their kiss that changes their frog into a prince. Their love is supposed to transform *his* life, then *theirs*.

Why not start with transforming your own life, then see if he is inspired to transform his own with your support? When you are a woman or a man who lives a life without excuses, the past and the present are no longer stumbling blocks, but stepping stones. The challenges in life don't weigh you down: they buoy you up.

It's like the story about the new preacher visiting her rural congregation in a beautiful valley for the first time. The luscious valley was the home of four magnificent farms. The preacher pulled up to the first farm, noticing the gleaming farmhouse with finely constructed buildings and beautiful flowers gardens surrounding it. Miles and miles of fencing surrounded all of these things, but it appeared that the fences were weather-worn and had gone without paint for a long time. When the concerned pastor inquired about the dilapidated fences the farmer replied that their state was caused by his workers. The only excuse he could offer was that it was a family-run farm and whenever family members argued with each other, they took their frustration out on the fencing.

The pastor went to visit the second farm. She saw fields uniformly tilled with cattle grazing nearby. The field looked well kept, but the cattle looked underfed. The field reflected tender loving care, while the cattle looked haggard and neglected. The concerned pastor asked the farmer about the discrepancy. The farmer said it was because of bad weather and poor health. As a newcomer to the valley, the farmer knew the preacher did not know that he had been in the hospital and that there was a drought going on. The farmer couldn't take care of both the fields and cattle in his condition, so he decided to take care of the fields.

The third farmer had acres of orchards with beautiful, mature apple and peach trees. The leaves were bright and the fruit was ripe and the limbs were laden with fruit waiting to be picked. The preacher asked about the unpicked fruit. The farmer knew that the preacher didn't know his mother had died when he was young and that his father had run off with somebody else. He was raised by a succession of relatives, family, friends, and strangers. He often suffered bouts of depression as a result of his childhood, and sometimes it was hard to get things going. The trees stood with their fruit rotting on the limbs.

The preacher finally arrived at the fourth farm. This farmer had immaculate buildings and facilities. The fences were freshly painted, surrounded by beautiful flowers. The fields were uniformly tilled and an impressive, healthy herd of cattle grazed nearby. The peach and apple trees were laden with fruit, and workers were climbing up and down the ladders bringing down boxes of ripe fruit. The preacher asked the farmer how he was doing. The farmer knew that the preacher did not know that he had had a lousy childhood; or that his family, who ran the farm, had been feuding every day; or that he had had surgery the previous month; and that the drought nearly killed all of his cattle. The farmer said, "I trust God to supply all my needs." The preacher told the farmer that surely God had blessed him with a magnificent farm. The farmer said that he was grateful and added, "You should have seen this place when God had it all by himself!"

The preacher drove back to town thinking that each farmer was blessed with the same good land, each had the same opportunities, each had problems, each struggled with circumstances past and present, beyond their control. Three of the farmers used family, plus past and present events to justify poor performance and neglect of responsibility. The fourth farmer was grateful for what he had, and he did what he could with what he had. Three farmers used their excuses to absolve themselves. The fourth partnered with God to live beyond his excuses.

THERE ARE ALWAYS CHOICES TO BE MADE

Rachel and Paulette decided to use their excuses in different ways to help, not hinder, themselves. Paulette changed her focus to an area that was more realistic in view of her current health condition, rather than completely giving up on life. Rachel could have used her rocky start in life as an excuse for everything that went wrong the rest of her life. But she had insight and was aware of her issues and this allowed her to retrieve and retrospect. Through the personal transformation of Living Water Rachel turned her life into a beautiful fountain, using her energy to help those still caught in the stagnant water of excuses.

You may not choose when or how you will die, but you can choose how you spend eternity. You don't choose when or how a child or spouse dies, but you can choose how you remember their living. The Kennedy family chose to celebrate the sudden death of John Kennedy, Jr., wife Carolyn, and sister-in-law Lauren with memorial services celebrating their lives, instead of bemoaning their losses. You may not have chosen your eye color, but you can change it. You may not have chosen the color of your hair, its texture, or length, but you can color it, cover it with a wig, weave, extend, straighten, curl, cut, or shave it. You may not have chosen your hips, lips, breasts, or buttocks, but whatever God didn't give you, Flai Roberts Fashion Fair, Frederick of Hollywood, Nordstrom's, or Victoria's Secret can. You may not have chosen the trials that incapacitate you, but you can choose how you respond to them. You may not have chosen physical liabilities, but you can choose not to let them invalidate your life. You may not have chosen your failures, but you can choose whether to lie where you fall or get up to fight another day. You did not choose the sins of others even though they impact your life, but Jesus came to heal the brokenhearted and set the captives free (Isaiah 61:1–3). You may not have intended to fall in the face of temptation, but there is a balm in Gilead to soothe the sin-sick soul.

Jesus gave us the power to choose. As the woman at the well discovered, we can never be successful or experience transformation while remaining victimized by excuses. She could never be free while remaining victimized by her past and current circumstances. She now had the power to decide whether to live like a beggar or a chooser. Begging women take whatever and whoever comes along. They go begging for acceptance and approval, begging for security, intimacy, and safety from the first available resource. They are not too careful about what they get—as long as they get something or someone—because they have unhealthy senses of self-worth. Begging women do not believe they are ever good enough, so they scrounge around for what they can find. Begging women journey through life concerned about how others see them, so they rearrange who they really are to suit others. They change clothes, hairstyles, taste, opinion, personality, and where and when they draw their daily supply of water. Since they are more concerned with whether they are liked, or whether others want to be with them, they shift their shapes to accommodate others' needs. The Samaritan woman begged through five relationships, and was cohabiting with another. It was the culturally acceptable way for a desperate woman to have food, clothing, and shelter, but it was not beneficial. Shame and guilt separated her from her community. "Everything is permissible"—but not everything is beneficial. "Everything is permissible"—but not everything is constructive" (1 Corinthians 10:23).

Women of choice examine their options. They look to see if what is permissible is beneficial and constructive. If something fails the test, they are secure enough to push the eject button. Choosing women do not throw away the sacred for temporal satisfaction. They do not throw their pearls to a swine; that is to say, they do not give precious gifts to those who mistreat those gifts. Women of choice choose to have the presence of Christ in their lives. They exercise their choices by trusting the Lord, instead of depending only on their own intellect, intuition, wisdom, and understanding (Proverbs 3:5–6). Women who exercise the power of choice realize they cannot do everything or be everything to everyone all the time. They ascribe to the "women who do too much" three-D choice method: dropping, delaying, and delegating. Women of choice are not ruled by the tyranny of tasks. They ask, "Is this a priority?" If the answer is no, they drop the task. They ask, "Does this have to be done now?" If the answer is no, they delay. They ask, "Must this be done by me personally?" If the answer is no, they delegate the responsibility.

There are a fourth and fifth D, I like to add. One is deny. Women of choice would ask, "Is this beneficial, constructive, and will it honor the Lord, Jesus Christ?" If the answer is no, they deny it. The other D is discern. In the presence of Christ, the Samaritan woman was able to discern that this stranger would not harm her. She discerned that the confrontation was to help her not to harm her, and when she blurted in confession Jesus did not condemn her, but liberated her. Discernment ushers in wisdom, insight, and understanding beyond human mental faculties. It is wise to know that every smile is not real and every frown is not sour; every friend is not a friend and every enemy can be transformed into a friend. It is wise to know when to rein it in or let it all hang out. Wisdom knows the value of starting early or starting over. It knows when to hold on and when to let go. Wisdom knows not to take yourself too seriously, and that laughter is good medicine for the soul. Discernment is the wisdom to know what to run from, and where and who to turn to. It's insight that sees past the superficial and right into the heart of every matter. Discernment does not come with maturity; it comes from a relationship with Jesus who holds the past, present, and future in his hands. In the presence of Christ, we too can make the choices that enhance our living. We can make a decision to become a chooser, and not a beggar.

Annika had been assigned a project at work that seemed to her to be beyond the scope of what she was capable of doing. Several others in her department had already turned the project down, and Annika could think of some perfect excuses that would relieve her of the chore also. Instead, she decided to be proactive about her circumstances. She sought to use her excuses as bridges rather than gaping chasms. Rather then let herself be overwhelmed by the enormity of the assignment, she asked God to partner with her in succeeding. She broke the project down into smaller projects, did what she could with what she had and trusted God for the wisdom to accomplish the rest. She did not make excuses. She made decisions. She worked hard and refused to let anyone take away her potential, turning the project into a liberating opportunity of strength training and success.

The Samaritan woman was now free from the excuses that tied her decision-making patterns to habit, history, and heritage. When her first relationship failed, she had an excuse available. It established a pattern that replicated itself six times in her life. She was in the rut of habitual relationship catastrophe, and she always had an excuse to justify to herself and others why things kept working out the way they did. Listen to her voice: "It's not working out, because it never works out. They treat me this way because I am not good enough; five men have said so. There is something about me that keeps attracting the same kind of men into my life. I must not be good enough because if I were, things would be better." The Samaritan woman has broken out of anonymity to confront the issues of her past. She is no longer held hostage by past mistakes, and after her encounter with the Divine at the well she is no longer a spectator, but the birth mother of new possibilities. She is well on her way down the road of her transformation.

CALL TO ACTION

Change only takes place with personal involvement, personal investment, and personal reflection. The difference between success and failure is often how you use what happens to you in life. Impoverished people left with only pieces of a hog turn pigtails, knuckles, ears, tongue, and feet into gourmet delicacies. Women left with only tattered pieces of cloth turn them into quilts to keep their families warm. George Washington Carver took the lowly peanut and developed the research that supported the founding of an industry. Used clothing is recycled through nearly new shops. One person's garbage is sold at swap meets and flea markets; it is the "if you get a lemon make lemonade" routine. For the Samaritan woman, the invitation to return and reflect upon her past freed her from excuses. Her future was greater than anything in her past; what was in front of her was greater than what was behind. Do not use yesterday's mistakes as an excuse not to move forward into the future.

For many women, excuses have become internalized to such an

extent that they function as limitations on our lives, which become controlled by unspoken fears within. They are the boundaries we have decided to live within, and if not examined carefully, become the context defining how far we dare to go in life. Focusing on the positive and not allowing oneself to be held back by limitations opens up a whole new world. The Samaritan woman came to the well with lots of excuses and all of her excuses were very good. However, she was there in part because of poor decisions. At those critical times when we are challenged about why we have settled into stagnant waters, when we have been offered Living Water, we can pull out our excuses or reach for an opportunity. Don't allow yourself to be held back by limitations. Instead of waiting for things to get better, make a list of all the things you can do until your situation changes.

Discipline of the Well

Well Lesson

Daughters of the well, the first Well Lesson is to stop making excuses, and start making decisions. If you continue to be ruled by excuses, as the Samaritan woman was, you will never be successful or experience transformation. The decision to live a decisive life frees you to be selective. The power of choice is now in your hands. You will choose whether to quit or finish. You will choose to do what you can with what you have, for nothing is impossible to God (Philippians 4:13). Women of choice take a careful look at their options, then ask and trust God to give them wisdom and understanding.

The second Well Lesson is that it's not what we have that matters, it's what we do with what we have. Live beyond limitations. Remember the four farmers who were given the same assets and the same liabilities? Based on their attitudes toward life, only one took the bull by the horns and lived a full and complete life without excuses. Eliminating excuses is a liberating experience. Even when your problems remain the same, you perceive life in a different light when your attitude changes. Attitude makes all the difference. Choose to live above your circumstances, rather than under them.

The third lesson from the well is that there are always choices to be made. From sunrise to sundown you make thousands of choices every day. You did not choose the time of your birth, or who your parents were, or your siblings, but you can choose how you relate to them. God gave you the power to choose. You cannot change other people; you can only change yourself. The next time you are about to relate to someone, think about how you will communicate. It's all about choices. You get to choose.

Well Words

This day I call heaven and earth as witnesses against you that I have set before you life and death, blessings and curses. Now choose life, so that you and your children may live.

DEUTERONOMY 30:19

You did not choose me, but I chose you and appointed you to go and bear fruit—fruit that will last. Then the Father will give you whatever you ask in my name.

JOHN 15:16

But God chose the foolish things of the world to shame the wise; God chose the weak things of the world to shame the strong.

1 CORINTHIANS 1:27

But you are a chosen people, a royal priesthood, a holy nation, a people belonging to God, that you may declare the praises of him who called you out of darkness into his wonderful light.

1 PETER 2:9

For the wages of sin is death, but the gift of God is eternal life in Christ Jesus our Lord.

ROMANS 6:23

Choose my instruction instead of silver, knowledge rather than choice gold.

PROVERBS 8:10

Trust in the Lord with all your heart, and lean not on your own understanding; in all your ways acknowledge him, and he will make your paths straight.

PROVERBS 3:5–6

"Everything is permissible"—but not everything is beneficial. "Everything is permissible"—but not everything is constructive.

1 CORINTHIANS 10:23

Well Sabbatical

⁓ Take your sabbatical outside. Take a walk in the park, a leisurely stroll in a garden, or take a stroll where you can enjoy the sights and sounds of nature. Take the time to enjoy a sunrise or a sunset for a change.

⁓ Record in your journal what you saw, smelled, or touched. Don't make excuses: Make a decision to find the time for this outdoor sabbatical. Fresh air works in an amazing way to clear our thinking. Movement increases the flow of oxygen to the blood. Circulation increases the flow to the brain. A change of scenery sometimes gives us a new perspective, as we get up-close and personal in our own lives. We need to shut off and push back from the daily in-office, in-home, or inside routines of lives.

It wouldn't hurt to bring the outdoors indoors. Buy fresh flowers for yourself or purchase a living plant. Light a fire in the fireplace, if you have one. Otherwise, boil fresh cinnamon sticks or a drop of pine oil in hot water on the stove; the aroma is fresh and delicious. Open the doors and windows where you live or work to let fresh air in for a while.

Be still, breathe deeply, and listen for the still small voice of God. Breathe, listen, and write what the Spirit tells you to write in your journal.

Well Language

- You are capable.
- It is within your reach.
- The Lord will be your helper.
- Nothing beats a try.
- I make decisions not excuses.
- I am a chooser, not a beggar.

Well Work

1. Face up to one of your excuses. We have lived with our excuses for too long. We have taken them everywhere, packed carefully in our backpacks and briefcases, hauling them from one event to the next. Facing the truth of our excuses can be a painful process, but in the presence of Christ, we can identify them. Jesus is a patient deity who will methodically peel the layers of

excuses away until we receive our power to choose. That is not to say our forward progress will sometimes be impeded. It only means that we can choose how to respond to it, as an obstacle or as stepping-stones.

2. Brainstorm about at least one way to respond to an existing challenge in your life. Write in your journal your thoughts about what you can do until your situation changes. When you have completed one idea, move to the next. For example: Are you unemployed with time on your hands? You can sit and sulk at home or volunteer your time and talents at church or a non-profit organization. Does debt or bad credit burden you? Seek professional credit counseling before seeking a loan or more credit cards. This service is free in some areas. Cut up your credit cards and cut down your budget. Make the decision to do those things that lead to debt-free living.

3. Write in your journal a list of things you can do until change comes.

10
A Woman Takes an Opportunity

"Sir," the woman said, "I can see that you are a prophet. Our fathers worshiped on this mountain, but you Jews claim that the place where we must worship is in Jerusalem." Jesus declared, "Believe me, woman, a time is coming when you will worship the Father neither on this mountain nor in Jerusalem."

JOHN 4:19-21

*H*elene lived with whatever came her way, whether it was a job, a man, or a friendship. She believed that if something presented itself it was an opportunity to be taken. Consequently, she ended up in many counterproductive pursuits going wherever the wind blew her. She was heading for her third divorce, didn't talk to her mother and sisters, hated her job, and had lost track of the two young children she and a boyfriend had together before her latest marriage. She thought they were living with his sister. A friend had gotten into trouble and needed to borrow money, and as a friend Helene felt compelled to help. Trouble is it was a lot of money and now the "friend" has skipped town. To raise the money Helene maxed out her credit limits and is in deep debt. She thought she was making the most of life by going with the flow and reacting to life as it happened around her. What she couldn't figure out was if God didn't mean for her to become involved in these situations, then why did God present them in her life?

Six men had presented the Samaritan woman with the opportunity to live together, and each one of them used and abused her. Because of circumstances within her culture, the Samaritan woman had drifted along until she was down to her last things with only one hope and a community of citizens that gossiped about her and looked upon her with scorn. Now she found herself traveling to the well during the hottest part of the day just to avoid them.

In this chapter, you'll clarify the truth about how you are influencing and shaping the person you are becoming when, like the Samaritan woman who met Jesus at the well, you too are presented with teachable moments and opportunities every day, both expected and unexpected. You can choose to continue going to the well at the wrong time of day or you can recognize opportunities as liberating experiences. Be aware.

NURTURING OPPORTUNITIES

An opportunity is a new situation that can produce new results. Possibilities abound. Opportunities lie at the crossroads of God's grace, God's will, and God's destiny, and like grace they can't be earned, purchased, bought, or sold, but are given. Like jewels, opportunities can be precious and rare, and when they are valuable they become priceless treasures. In *Wake Up Your Dreams*, Dr. Walt Kallestad writes that there are opportunities we make happen, opportunities that are discovered while we are doing something else, and opportunities that lead to other opportunities. Living Water is an opportunity itself. Jesus can bring us beyond the leftover crumbs society has to offer.

Helene was not responding to opportunities. She was reacting to the leftover crumb situations that presented themselves. Just because a circumstance presented itself did not mean it was an opportunity to be taken. There is a big difference between an opportunity and leftover crumbs; Helene needed a transforming experience to figure out the difference.

An opportunity is a lot like handling an egg—the reproductive receptacle produced by various hosts including reptiles, birds, dinosaurs, and some mammals such as humans. Handle the egg carelessly, and the precious substance within it will be wasted. Apply too much pressure to the egg, and it will be crushed. Nurture the egg with warmth and security in a proper environment, and it might hatch. Trust it to those who are experts in egg handling, and it might turn into something greater. Turn the heat up too quickly, and it will crack. Intentionally crack it, mix it, blend it with other ingredients, and create the best omelet in the world. Just as there are different kinds of eggs, there are also different kinds of opportunities. Opportunities are produced by a variety of hosts including events, circumstances, and people, both planned and unexpected. Mishandle a raw opportunity and you could have a mess on your hands. Opportunities mixed with other ingredients and a good recipe will blend in skills, special talents, education, contacts, courage, and the grace of God. Incubate the egg for three weeks, and you just might hatch a chicken, which will produce even more delectable egg opportunities.

The Samaritan woman was surprised that while fetching water she was presented with an opportunity. She had no time to prepare for the opportunity she encountered, no letter of invitation, prior telephone calls, or faxes. She was alone at the well, without mentor, coach, or employer. Alone with Jesus, and she had the opportunity to take the next step toward personal transformation. Personal transformation begins with acts of personal revelation, which has two distinct components. The first component is the personal revelation of God, which enables the second component, personal revelation of self, a face-to-face revelation with truths that transform.

It is impossible to have a true vision of self without a true vision of God. The prophet Isaiah saw God at the death of King Uzziah. The revelation of God fostered a revelation of self. Isaiah declared, "'Woe to me!' I cried. 'I am ruined! For I am a man of unclean lips, and I live among a people of unclean lips, and my eyes have seen the King, the Lord Almighty'" (Isaiah 6:5). Moses acknowledged his weaknesses when he saw God in a burning bush. Who would believe an accused murderer, who was slow to speak, and brought up in Pharaoh's house by an unwed foster mother? (Exodus 2:9–10) Peter saw the extraordinary power of Jesus Christ in the miracles of fishes and declared, "Go away from me Lord; I am a sinful man" (Luke 5:8).

The Samaritan woman all of a sudden realized that her journey to the well was not an ordinary chance meeting with a stranger. Spiritual implications were rushing through her mind. Jesus was not an ordinary man offering ordinary water. Her belief systems were being challenged and all the sordid details of a promiscuous lifestyle were flashing before her eyes like dust rising in a storm, dust that could no longer be swept under the rug or hidden in the closet. She confronted the truth of who she was. The woman of Samaria saw herself, and so did this stranger at the well who dared to reveal to her the secrets and truths of her life. How could this man know the details of her private life? She stood vulnerable, uncovered, and exposed in his presence. The only place of escape had become a place of personal transformation.

Much as the prodigal son came to himself on the pig farm in a far away country, or how Zaccheus confronted himself while Jesus dined at his house one day, the woman at the well confronted herself at Jacob's well. It's much the same way the thief hanging next to Jesus on the cross confronted himself; the judgment was passed, but he seized the opportunity presented to him by a forgiving Christ to spend eternity in Paradise. This was no ordinary man, this prophet of opportunity.

CHANGING THE SUBJECT

How would the Samaritan woman handle this opportunity? She changed the subject. How often do we change the subject in the midst of an uncomfortable conversation? Jesus was getting too close for comfort, and she deflected the probing into her personal life. We have all known people who can expertly extricate themselves from revealing conversations. They have learned how to avoid answering those self-incriminating personal questions. They know how to distract others with conversation to hide behind the smokescreens of trivial discussions. Sometimes we ourselves have borrowed a page from the book of tactical maneuvers on avoidance. We've started arguments because we didn't want to talk about a problem, accused others of things not relevant to the discussion, blamed others for anything rather than engage in personal revelation, and we have cut conversations short or walked away from encounters that caused us to see ourselves or face issues we'd rather avoid. We can talk about the weather, death, taxes, economic indicators, rocket science, religion, or anything other than the truth about ourselves, which we avoid diligently. We can spend years dodging the subjects of self and life. Artful dodgers proclaim, "No one really knows who I am!" But then, neither do they. The woman at the well began a discussion about old controversies between the Jews and the Samaritans: "Our fathers worshiped on this mountain, but you Jews claim that the place where we must worship is in Jerusalem" (John 4:20).

Instead of taking a real look at opportunities in her life, Helene changed the subject and put the focus on God. Why would God allow such situations to be put in front of her if she wasn't supposed to embrace them? Even though she had not been including God in her life choices, she justified her behavior by blaming God. She dodged the real issue and denied that she could possibly be held responsible or accountable.

The Samaritan woman changed the subject and began asking questions about where to worship. The Samaritans tampered with history and religion. They believed that Mount Gerizim was the place to gain access to God through worship and sacrifice. It was there they believed Abraham was willing to sacrifice his only son Isaac, where the priest Melchizedek appeared to Abraham, and where Moses made sacrifices when the Hebrews first entered into the Promised Land. The place where Moses made sacrifices was on Mount Ebal, not Mount Gerizim (Deuteronomy 27:4), and the Jews taught that Jerusalem was the sacred place to gain access to God. The Samaritan woman's response may have been a sincere inquiry about where to worship and offer sacrifices. Her response shows that she was seeking forgiveness for the sins she had just acknowledged. The woman at the well wanted to know where she should worship God. Jesus didn't deny her worship nor disqualify her from worship. Jesus told her the day was coming when the location of worship wouldn't matter. A new era was dawning. The old regime of patriarchal and hierarchical glory of the old covenant was being reshaped, controversies that separated God's people would diminish, and a new covenant was being written in the blood of the Lamb. Access to God was for anyone at anytime. Authentic worship finds God anywhere.

TEACHABLE MOMENTS

It was at the well that this woman was faced with an opportunity created by what Howard Thurman would call a teachable moment. A teachable moment is a crack in your armor through which God penetrates your life. Such things as crises, disappointments, pain, and even sudden and unexpected encounters with God create these moments. A teachable moment occurs when circumstances force you to look outside yourself. To look past knowledge or former coping strategies that have failed or were inadequate. It is when your belief system is in danger of failing, and you are made ready to hear from God. You begin to take stock during teachable moments. You realize that what you thought you knew is no longer enough. Questions emerge such as: Who are you and where are you going now? What have you been doing, and what are you going to do now?

Before you seize a teachable moment, the desire for change is weak, and the need for change is often not a clear, or a pressing, priority. If you can continue to get by just the way you are, who needs change? It's the "if it's not broken why fix it?" routine. You have fallen asleep in the "do not disturb" dust of the past. You don't learn from your teachable moments at other times because your defense mechanisms want to maintain the status quo, even if it's negative. Before the teachable moment arrives, you resist change. The door of your fool's paradise is locked tight. Culture, tradition, religion, and social pressure cannot budge the door an inch. Now, the door is flung wide open and you are ready to learn, grow, and change. Suddenly things become clear, insight and understanding flood your consciousness, and the need for pretense evaporates like water in the desert sun. It is the moment of self-revelation. You wake up wondering why you do what you do, go where you go, take what you take, and give what you have been giving. Suddenly you become conscious of your present reality and wonder why you have wasted so many years doing something you have no business doing. It's the wake-up call that startles you out of your comatose state. At the onset of the teachable moment, some women wake up wondering what they have been doing for the last twenty years, as if they fell asleep at puberty and woke up at menopause. Teachable moments bring bad behaviors to the surface and weaknesses become visible as your cover erodes. Faulty thinking can no longer be justified.

· Helene's wall of defense began to crumble. She began to see that the choices she had been making were not made with discernment and that God needed to be a part of the equation. Her life was not working, and a new awareness of teachable moments prepared her to learn as her mind became attentive and ready to acquire, process, and analyze new knowledge and information.

Just as you must be vigilant to see the Divine in the ordinary moments of your life, you must also be vigilant to the teachable moment opportunities. To take full advantage of teachable moments you must remember to be vigilant in recognizing opportunities when they come along. Many opportunities slip through your fingers because you fail to notice them as opportunities. You remove yourself from the middle of things, where opportunities are most plentiful. Instead you are content in the margins, on the fringes, or with the leftover crumbs assigned to you. Too often when an encounter comes along at your own Samaritan well you can't believe that it's happening; you feel you don't deserve it or haven't earned it. You feel as if you're not worthy of it, and so you miss it, and once an opportunity is lost it cannot be retrieved. You cannot bring back yesterday. Your own stumbling blocks keep you from realizing opportunities when you avoid close encounters and risk. It takes risk, courage, and effort to put yourself in a position that creates opportunities.

Moses went out of his way while keeping sheep in the Median desert to climb the mountain to see the burning bush. The bush did not come to him. Elijah left the cave to stand on the edge of the mountain to hear the still small voice of God. David went to Goliath. Esther went to see the king. Deborah went into battle. And Bill Gates wasn't sitting around avoiding new computer applications—he developed them. Jesus intentionally met the Samaritan woman in the midst of an ordinary trip to the well.

Opportunities are lost because too often women are afraid. They are afraid that opportunities may mean a change they're not ready for. They are afraid that opportunities may separate them from what they know, or who they are. They are afraid that the revelation of God and self may separate them from their current relationships. Some women are afraid of change, even change for the better. They are so used to negative energies and lifestyles that they are unwilling to do the hard work of investing themselves in positive life changes, even temporarily. It was easy for the Samaritan woman to engage in relationship roulette—she had to have someone to support and protect her. However, she lacked respect, intimacy, and dignity, and was left feeling empty and alone.

A kind-hearted person, Helene needed to get herself down to the nearest well for a teachable moment before she got excited about another "opportunity." Helene was not clear on what was meaningful in her life, she had no sense of purpose and she needed to look into the eyes of Jesus and have a serious conversation with God on facing her past, excuses, and overcoming learned ignorance. She was desperately in need of a personal transformation. She certainly did not know about kairos moments yet, but she was about to learn.

Learning disabilities, conditions that make it a challenge for people to achieve learning, keep some women from accomplishing personal revelation. Some conditions can be handled so that learning is achieved through specialized curriculums, classes, schools, and medical resources. In life, learning disabilities can also be conditions that keep us from accomplishing a clear vision of God and self. Fear, low self-esteem, past experiences, cultural, societal, and historical definitions, pride, arrogance, stubbornness, guilt, shame, and sin can incapacitate our ability to learn, and so we live our lives in a catatonic state, a mental and spiritual stupor. We get up every morning and go to our Samaritan's well, avoiding everyone, including ourselves, to take care of the necessities of life. God will intentionally meet us at our Samaritan wells to help us overcome our learning disabilities. The perfect love of God casts out fear (1 John 4:18). God did not give us a spirit of fear, but he did give us a spirit of power, love, and a sound mind (2 Timothy 1:7). God created us in the image of the Divine, and we are fearfully and wonderfully made (Genesis 2–3; Psalm 139). Everyone who asks shall be redeemed (Romans 10:13). And, in our new relationship with Christ, we become transformed (2 Corinthians 5:17).

The Samaritan woman's barriers had crumbled; there was nothing between her soul and the Savior. Personal revelation could now occur. The Samaritan woman had an opportunity. Could she overcome her learning disabilities or would she retreat to the way things had always been? Would she climb the stairs built by "possibility" to look out the windows that "potential" had opened? Or would she remain in the cellar of her painful past? She could do nothing about her yesterdays, but she could do something about the rest of her life, seizing the opportunity to wake up to the reality of God and herself, seen by the dawn's early light breaking forth over the horizon of her character and lifestyle. She suddenly saw herself in the presence of Jesus by the well and sought only to worship and sacrifice. Many times opportunities come when we least expect them. When Jesus came to the well and exposed her past life, he created an opportunity for redemption even though the Samaritan woman was not seeking it. He did not meet her to reprimand her, nor affirm her shady lifestyle. He entered her life to remove the barriers between her and God. A marginal member of the community now had access to God, foreshadowing the coming work of the cross. Such old elements of exclusion as race, gender, and heritage had no validity when Jesus affirmed her value and worth as being separate from her history and womb. Her confession paved the way for a teachable moment, and her life of avoidance disappeared. Self-revelation can be a rude awakening; allow it to lead you to seek out God, a greater source outside yourself. God breaks through, and what God has been trying to say to us, we are finally ready to hear. God breaks into your life so you can see yourself reflected in divine eyes. As you begin to examine the truth about yourself in a protected environment of the secret place of the Most High, the truth about self can be a liberating experience. The meaning of your life, and who and what is meaningful in your life, becomes clear.

The Jews believed that women did not have souls. They were forbidden Torah instruction and were not counted in the quorum necessary for worship, the minyan, or allowed into ancient rabbinical schools. Jesus engaged the Samaritan woman in a theological discussion of ancient rivalries during an era when men didn't speak to women in public, let alone discuss religious issues. The gender condemned in the Garden of Eden is affirmed at the well. She met more than a man who spent time with her and patiently helped her work through some issues. At the well she met a man who talked about something other than cell phones, automobiles, computers, and sex. She met a man who shared his concerns and heard hers. Jesus skipped over issues of cultural prejudices, social segregation, and racial purity and talked to her about theological issues. He thought more of her than anyone had in a long time. There are still women today who believe they are not worth the time of day. Jesus comes to our well experiences to remind us we are women of worth and that there is a woman of value and worth inside each of us. Stop throwing your life away. Stop taking the low road because you believe you are not good enough for the high road. Stop accepting the leftover crumbs society has to offer. Jesus offers Living Water to all daughters of value and worth, and that includes you. Watch for opportunities in your life. Spend some time with God focusing on increasing your sense of who God is and what God can do.

CALL TO ACTION

You have an opportunity: You can overcome your learning disabilities or you can retreat to the way things have always been. You have a choice: There is nothing you can do about yesterday, but there is something you can do about the rest of your life, seizing the opportunity to wake up to the reality of God. Take a good look at your character and lifestyle. See yourself in the presence of Jesus by the well. Like the Samaritan woman, you can choose to move beyond the roadblocks in your life. Barriers will crumble when there is nothing between your soul and the Savior, and personal revelation will take place. Take a good look at the opportunities in your life; make the most of God-given opportunities, not every thing that comes along like Helene.

Shaun made a decision to leave her job to start her own business. She'd made a lot of money for other people now she believed God was telling her to move out into her own accounting business. She moved quickly through the doors the Lord had opened for her to obtain reasonable office space, start-up money and a few faithful clients. On her last day at the firm she was leaving, her boss offered to a "too good to be true" job. She was offered her own department handling only corporate accounting clients. The title, vice president, and raise alone made her heart pound!

She spent additional time with God at her personal well. In the end, Shaun turned down the promotion. She was clear about which opportunity was God sent. A year later, the new department was dismantled, the new vice president and accountants fired as the company downsized. Shaun was doing great with all the new business in her own company from her old clients! Sometimes, choices are presented so that you become clear about the decisions you've made.

Take a deep breath and be determined to take advantage of every opportunity and every teachable moment, running toward the opportunities, instead of away from them.

Discipline of the Well

Well Lesson

Women of opportunity, our first Well Lesson is that the Devine encourages you to nurture the right opportunities. You cannot have a true vision of self without first having a true vision of God. Personal transformation begins when you have a personal revelation of God and a personal revelation of self; these are the two truths that challenge your belief systems. Keep excuses and changing the subject out of the picture so that you do not have to live just an ordinary life, but can live extraordinarily.

The second lesson from the well is that the Living Water Jesus provides brings you beyond the leftover crumbs society has to offer. Be empowered by the power of God to step over the barriers that have crumbled and make the most of every opportunity. Sometimes opportunities come of a crisis but keep your eyes open to the teachable moments taking shape. Move beyond the limitations holding you back from your dreams.

Our third Well Lesson is that acknowledging your strengths and weaknesses, reviewing your belief systems, and becoming aware of the kairos moments create teachable moments in your every day experiences. Opportunities can be teachable moments and teachable moments can become opportunities. Make the most of every teachable moment. Breathe deeply into your soul and be determined to take advantage of every opportunity.

The fourth lesson is that just as Jesus spoke it at the well, the time is here, even in this post-Resurrection twenty-first century to worship the Lord privately, publicly, anytime, anyplace, and anywhere.

Well Words

Let the morning bring me word of your unfailing love, for I have put my trust in you. Show me the way I should go, for to you I lift up my soul.

PSALM 143:8

Teach me to do your will, for you are my God; may your good spirit lead me on level ground.

PSALM 143:10

You women who are so complacent, rise up and listen to me; you daughters who feel secure, hear what I have to say!

ISAIAH 32:9

The tongue has the power of life and death, and those who love it will eat its fruit.

PROVERBS 18:21

My ears had heard of you but now my eyes have seen you.

JOB 42:5

Therefore, as we have opportunity, let us do good to all people, especially to those who belong to the family of believers.

GALATIANS 6:10

... because a great door for effective work has opened to me, and there are many who oppose me.

1 CORINTHIANS 16:9

Well Sabbatical

⌐ Spend a portion of your regular rest and reflection period, or one entire sabbatical per week, asking God to open your eyes to opportunities found along the pathway of living, the unexpected surprises missed while looking for the pot of gold at the end of the rainbow. Partner with God to seize, nurture, and make the most of all opportunities: the ones you go after, the ones you make happen, and the ones God's grace and God's will send your way. Look for ways to use one opportunity as a bridge to another.

⌐ Spend moments in your sabbatical looking toward the horizon for new opportunities; not mourning the ones you missed, messed up, or ignored, but eagerly grasping those opportunities before you.

Well Language

⌐ I am worth it!
⌐ I am valuable!
⌐ I am becoming.
⌐ I have the courage to pursue God's opportunities.
⌐ I am open to new possibilities everyday.
⌐ Problems are opportunities in disguise.
⌐ Lord, I am ready to learn, grow and live. Teach me!
⌐ I am awake now!

Well Work

1. *Take a few moments each day and look in the mirror. The look is not to adjust your halo, lipstick, hair, or check for crow's feet, wrinkles, or lines. Look yourself in the eye and see the woman staring back at you. What do your eyes tell you? If you were a stranger looking into those eyes what would your eyes tell you about this woman in the mirror? Do your eyes dance with laughter? Can you see the depth of your character? Are your eyes frightened like those of a deer confronted by a hunter? Are your eyes sad? Do they reflect pain or are they clouded by confusion? What do you see when you look yourself in the eye?*

2. *Record your impressions in your journal.*

3. *Look through magazines and newspapers for pictures of eyes that remind you of your eyes. Cut them out and place them on your collage.*

4. *Now, look yourself in the eye and tell yourself the things you need to hear, but no one is saying. There is no law that says you can't say them to yourself. I'm worth it! I am valuable to God! I am loved! I am blessed! This is going to be a blessed day! Words have power. Do not wait for someone else to speak what you need to hear. Life and death proceed from your mouth. Speak life today; speak those things that your spirit craves.*

5. *Write in your journal about your own teachable moments.*

II
A Woman of Value and Worth

You've been in a dark room for a long time. You didn't like the darkness at first, but your eyes adjusted to it. The opportunity to turn on the light was always there. You had the capacity to turn it on, you knew where the light switch was, and you had everything you needed to do it, you just had not thought of doing it. The idea that you could turn on the light had not been revealed to you. Suddenly, like dawning sunlight skipping across the shine of early morning dew, a thought not your own skips across your mind chasing darkness. A revelation happens. You turn on the light. You are compelled to flip the switch. When you do, the light chases the dark away; there is a light in the dark. You think this is too simple? You could have done this a long time ago, but the solution had not been revealed yet. The thought that turning on the light will end the darkness is a revelation. The thought may have been there all the time, but its importance was only revealed when you were ready to act on it. Turning on the light is the response to the revelation. Standing in a changed environment that signifies a changed reality is the fruit of the revelation. Revelation is not turning on the light when in the darkness. It is thought that by doing this action the problem can be solved.

Revelation is the idea that took center stage on your mind. Revelation is a God-sent idea, moment, or thought. It may be an answer to a question, a solution to a question that leads to other questions and solutions, or a thought that makes clear the cloudy. It is a light in the dark.

The Samaritan woman lived in the dark for a long time. She was tested over and over again. She had been living in unhealthy relationships for so long that she was ready to hit bottom. In fact, when she did hit bottom, she found that it was solid. It was there, at the bottom, in the dark, that she was able to experience a personal revelation of God and a personal revelation of self. Only then was she ready for personal transformation. Only then did she meet Jesus at the well that hot, sunny noonday in Samaria.

This chapter shows us how we, like the Samaritan woman, are valuable women of worth with the opportunity to take the next step of personal transformation, as many have said, our test becomes our testimony. Often, it is when our strength runs out, when we are down to our last things, that transformation becomes possible. We are finally at a point where we call upon God's strength instead of our own, to be led by the Holy Spirit instead of being led by our own inclinations, and to seek God first instead of relying only on human beings, including relying on only ourselves. Worship is the place where we can meet the Holy Spirit, where we can learn more about God, about ourselves, and about what we are capable of. Instead of failing the tests of life, we realize that our tests can become testimonies for God transforming us in ways we were not able to transform ourselves. Prepare to receive, women of value and worth.

CALL UPON GOD

Jesus preaches his first sermon not in a temple, but in a foreign land with a foreign woman. Imagine the scene: a holy hush around the sanctuary of the well. The surrounding mountains serve as walls, the sky a roof, and nature the interior decorator. The Chosen reaches for the soul of the rejected, planting within her the seed of messianic revelation and fulfillment. The cosmos leans forward as Jesus preaches his second sermon: "I am the Messiah." The world around them changes from anticipation of the Messiah to the arrival of the God who breaks into time and history through human flesh as the Word made flesh comes and dwells among us (John 1:14). During his sermon, Jesus trusts the revelation of Messiahship to a woman. He trusts vital spiritual revelation to a woman who couldn't get her relationship issues right. He opens up a vista of truth beyond amazement and wonder, witnessed only by her, the sand, sun, and holy ground of the well.

Worship is the opportunity to spend time in the presence and power of God. It is the means of transformation, a time when the immutable immortality of God meets the mortality of humankind in a personal revelation. It is an invitation to a special relationship where the weakness of humankind connects with the power of God. During worship, depression responds to healing, burdens are relieved, the helpless find help in times of trouble, and the stressed are strengthened. It is in worship that we learn more about God and find a new vision of what we can be and do. Worship leads to liberation and deliverance.

When the Samaritan woman challenged Jesus with questions, he answered her as if she were a disciple, a trained religious leader, or one of the men in the community. He spoke to her as an equal, affirming her intelligence and ability to understand spiritual matters. Jesus trusted the revelation of Messiahship to a woman deemed unworthy by both the Jews and Samaritans. He told her, "You Samaritans worship without knowing what you worship, but the time approaches, indeed is already here, when all true worshipers will worship the Father in spirit and in truth." Jesus reminds her that the Samaritans had an incomplete picture of God. When the Assyrians conquered the northern tribes of Israel, they brought their own gods with them and merely added the God Jehovah to their collection of gods, perhaps since Jehovah was the deity of the conquered territory. In other words, they were afraid not to worship the God of Israel and began to hold sacred the first five books of the Old Testament, discarding all the rest. Jewish rabbis had often charged the Samaritans with superstitious worship, worshiping not out of love and knowledge of God, but out of fear and superstition. It was a danger then, and it is a danger now.

We worship God in spirit and in truth, both corporately, with others, and privately, alone. It is a refreshing experience anytime, anywhere, for anyone on the path to personal revelation. The public and private worship of God, including prayer, fasting, praise, and sabbaticals, is a powerful place from which to hear God. We must listen for God through worship, not only listen to the TV for salvation. We do not worship inanimate objects, horoscopes, ourselves, our money, our tea leaves. He is a presence in our lives. God is more than a discipline but Divine. The message shared in Samaria at Jacob's well is that they who worship God worship him in spirit and in truth. The message shared at the foot of Mount Sinai after the liberation from Egypt is that we worship only God: "I am the Lord your God . . . You shall have no other gods before me" (Exodus 20:2–3). The message shared at Mount Carmel after the defeat of the four hundred prophets of Baal by the prophet Elijah is that "The Lord—he is God! The Lord—he is God!" (1 Kings 18:39). The message shared at Mount Calvary by a centurion at the foot of the cross while the earth shook and the sun refused to shine was "Surely he was the Son of God" (Matthew 27:54). The message shared at Mount Tabor spoken by God himself is that Jesus is God's Son, in whom he is well pleased. Listen to Him! (Matthew 17:5 or Mark 9:7), and on Mount Olivet, the message shared is that Jesus will return.

The call to worship is more than a call to duty and responsibility. In worship we reach with the expectation that we can touch the heart of God, in the name of Jesus, and be touched in return with personal revelation. Worship increases our sense of who God is and what God can do. As our spirit reaches for God's Spirit, it makes room for personal transformation to take place and teachable moments are created. We learn at this point in our journey to the well that our failures are not obstacles to worship. Jesus included rather than excluded the Samaritan woman. He made available to her what had been denied her because of gender, history, heritage, and habit. He met her particular needs by looking beyond her faults as she responded to the call to worship in spirit and in truth.

We still have trouble hearing the call to worship. Janice had been intending to fill the spiritual void in her life for several years—she just hadn't gotten around to figuring out how, so when her friend Jasmine invited her to a special worship service at her church she decided to go. The service was inspiring and spirit-led, and the people Janice met after the service seemed to have their lives really together. She wondered why Jasmine had so many friends with such a strong sense of purpose in life. It wasn't like they were perfect or anything, but compared to the crowd Janice hung out with they seemed to have such purpose and meaning in their lives. Most of Janice's friends had become disillusioned with religion a long time ago and had created their own forms of worship as in "I do not go to church, I worship God in my own way." Janice could tell they didn't have the same satisfaction in life she saw and felt in Jasmine's friends. She made a decision then and there to make this a weekly experience.

Today's generation may fall into fragmenting the Word of God based on its personal preferences and prejudices, adhering to a selective belief system. There are some that select a faith tradition in the same manner they select a mall to shop in. Which one can I get into and out of without a lot of time and commitment? Some are just like the Samaritans adding God to all the other idols and deities of the age. Jesus points to true worship. God is not wood, silver, or a golden object to be carried and placed in a protected area. God is Spirit, not confined to people, places, or things. God's presence is known, invisible yet immutable; unseen yet felt. As such, all believers can worship God in spirit and in truth. God is seeking those who are willing to engage the spirit in the pursuit of truth, willing to participate in an intimate relationship with a moral, invisible God who can meet us in the gardens of holy sanctuaries, the gardens of our bedrooms, the gardens of street corners, and the gardens of corporate and private worship. When the spirit of humankind soars to commune with God, genuine worship takes place. When the mortal, visible spirit of humankind rises to honor and glorify the immortal, invisible God who is spirit and truth, genuine worship takes place. The Holy Spirit deposits the visions of God into our spirits.

YOUR TEST BECOMES YOUR TESTIMONY

Tandia was a woman pursuing her revelation. Warren had always told his wife that he would help her dreams come true as she had helped him. They were married before he finished medical school, and Tandia worked a full-time job plus a part-time job until their income had reached a level that allowed them to achieve their goals: paying off school loans for both, purchasing cars, and putting a down payment on a home. Along the way four children arrived in rapid succession and Tandia's dreams were put on hold. The day arrived when the children were grown—had graduated or were in college—and finally, Tandia decided to pursue her dreams. She wanted to get a master's degree in business education, but that meant days in class and nights studying. Warren would have to help out more at home, plus they would have the additional expenses of tuition and books. She was starting a little later than most, Tandia thought, but better late than never. When she told Warren her plans he balked at the idea, thinking one professional in the family was enough. They both agreed that their income was at a level where she did not have to work, and Warren thought that her outside interests in charity and foundation work should be enough to fulfill her. But they weren't. Even though she realized that she would be close to retirement age when she completed her requirements, she had longed for a business degree since she was a little girl. Her dream, said Warren, would put a strain on their marriage. But Tandia reminded him that he always said one day it would be her turn. When was it going to be her turn?

Tandia put it in the hands of God. They always prayed together for each other's lives, careers, and family. After one morning personal-prayer meeting, ideas dropped into her spirit. She saw how they could readjust the family's finances. He could really take his day off to help with household responsibilities. Since he often worked late hours in the office and in surgery, Tandia could use that time to study. As Hannibal used to declare on the old television series *The A Team*: "I love it when a plan comes together!"

Tandia went to business school for her M.B.A. and graduated. Warren was blessed by seeing his wife's face as she received her diploma. This was a test, and they passed it. He'd never seen her look happier. Their relationship's test became the testimony; they found resilience in the face of change and remembered the importance of keeping one's promises. You are tested every day of your life. Life presents challenges that test our faith, strength, or self-esteem. An athlete's skill is tested in competition and an automobile's efficiency is tested on the road. You are tested when you hold your tongue when you wanted to speak at an in-appropriate time. You are tested when you want to eat what is not healthy for you. You are tested when you grow in grace and faith, even though it would be easier to succumb to the temptation of the secular. When your patience runs out you are tested to find some more, and when your strength runs out you are tested to call upon God's strength instead of your own. You are tested to be still instead of moving, to be led by the Holy Spirit instead of being led by your own inclinations, and to constantly seek God first instead of human experts in any field. These are all tests you face every day, and every time you pass a test it becomes a testimony, not for what you did personally, but for God's working out in you what you cannot do humanly yourself. God uses your circum-stances, good, bad, or indifferent, as an instructive lesson. Your desert wandering becomes fuel for the test, as many times you go to the well and return only with water. No change. No difference. No resolution. No relief. No revival. No miracle. No blessing. The test is to keep coming back. As Job declared, "Tho' he slay me, yet will I trust until my change comes." The test is in the journey, the trial is in the waiting and the testimony is the result of God's grace and power.

Jesus transformed water into wine at the wedding of Cana. He calmed the winds and the waves on the Sea of Galilee. He forgave the sins of a paraplegic in a house meeting in Capernaum. He fed thousands on the hillside with bread and fish, raised Lazarus from death to live at Bethany, but it was at Jacob's well that Jesus launched his ministry for lost souls. It was at this well that he revealed the redemptive work of the Messiah. He touched one woman's soul with Divine truth and opened the eyes of the returning disciples, who saw that the harvest of souls was at hand. The Samaritan woman was intuitive enough to seize the moment. Most of the time we are so busy with our own agendas that we are blind to the sacred breaking into ordinary moments of time. We are careless about what or whom we allow to take up God's space and time in our lives. It's as if we have time for everyone else except Jesus. As the disciples returned from the city they may have thought it was strange for Jesus to be speaking with the Samaritan woman, but they did not dare interrupt. Perhaps the power of the moment was still present, with virtue flowing and grace abounding. The disciples walked into the sanctuary of the well in the middle of the sermon and had enough sense to wait for a benediction. The entourage returned not knowing or fully understanding that Jesus had opened the doors of the church to everyone: every race, gender, and tribe. The salvation plan began with a select few and it now included the unthinkable, the untouchable, and the unworthy. Jesus had turned the tables. The last is now first to hear the messianic message. The least is now the one to return to the city to ignite a revival. The Samaritan woman was no longer on the fringes of history, she was now an intricate part of the salvation story.

WOMEN OF VALUE, WOMEN OF WORTH

The Samaritan woman was not expected to have any interests beyond hauling water. She wasn't supposed to have the intellect to handle spiritual questions. Yet the Samaritan woman was presented with the opportunity to take the next step toward personal transformation, which begins with acts of personal revelation. It was a teachable moment by the well and Jesus delivered two powerful revelations: The first is the personal revelation of God, which enables the second, the personal revelation of self, a face-to-face revelation with truths that transform. Teachable moments occur at kairos. They could be the result of shared experiences or personal crises. They may occur in the wake of achievements or on the heels of trial and tribulation. Teachable moments also occur in worship, prayer, and praise. God lowers the ego factor and removes all fear of success and failure, removes the avoidance tactic, and in an open moment reveals truths that we are more prone to get than at any other time.

Shema was pregnant for a second time. The first pregnancy went smoothly. She worked right up to her due date. This time was different. Her feet swelled. Her blood pressure shot up. She had morning sickness with a vengeance. Her doctor told her to stay off her feet, reduce her work load and go on an early maternity leave right away. Shema slowed down, but only a bit. She ignored the warning signs as simple fatigue. She kept her hectic schedule up until her water broke in the middle of a workday. Embarrassed, she was carried out of the office building on a stretcher leaving a pool of embryonic fluid at her desk. The baby arrived too early to survive.

It was her teachable moment. In the hours following the death of her baby, Shema understood the fragility of life. Life was not a guarantee but a gift to be treasured. Her life was not a burger from Burger King. She could not have it her way.

Jesus trusted the Samaritan woman with dramatic revelations and revealed to her that God is a Spirit and the Messiah. Can God trust you? Noah was trusted to build an ark, Solomon a temple, Josiah a revival, and Huldah with interpretation. John was trusted with a revelation on the isle of Patmos, Simeon and Anna were trusted to pray in the Jerusalem temple daily until they saw the Messiah. And they did. At times we have betrayed the Lord's trust. God trusted Jonah to take a message to Nineveh, and Jonah aborted the mission. After a detour in the belly of a great fish and a second call, Jonah finally carried out his mission. Peter was trusted to remain faithful, but he betrayed the Lord three times on the night of his trial. At times, we do the same. The mercy of the Lord gave Jonah a second chance. Peter was forgiven and told to go feed the sheep of Christ. That same mercy is available for us today.

CALL TO ACTION

The fruit of God's revelation is a blessing: You are blessed to be and blessed to do. It is a privilege and honor to partner with God in working your way out of challenges, crises, and critical issues. It is glorious to be in the presence of the mind of Christ, to have a glimpse of God's intention for the future and watch God go to work on it. It is also a burden, because this is a heavy responsibility. Obedience to God is required. The blessing involves stretching the spiritual muscles, tests of stamina, and strains of uncertainty that try your faith. New responsibilities always bring new tasks to shoulder. The Samaritan woman was available to the revelations of Christ. She was in a position to receive. Are you prepared to receive?

You've been in that dark room for a long time now. I know your eyes have adjusted to it, but do you really want to go on living in the darkness? The opportunity to turn on the light has always been there, and you have the capacity to do it. You know where the light switch is, and you have everything needed. Are you now ready to do something about your situation? A revelation can happen—you can turn on the light. Standing in a changed environment that signifies a changed reality is the fruit of the revelation.

Are you ready to turn on the light?

Discipline of the Well

Well Lesson

Our first Well Lesson is that spending time with Jesus is an experience in revelation. Worship increases your sense of who God is and what God can do. As you take the time to worship God, both corporately and privately, allow a holy hush to bring new insights, wisdom, and revelations. God is seeking those who are willing to worship the Lord with gladness, come before him with joyful songs. God is looking for those who can acknowledge that yes He is God. It is He who has made us and we are His. Enter His gates with Thanksgiving and into His courts with Praise. (Psalm 100:2–4). Call upon His name. Jesus opens the doors of worship to everyone; regardless of who they are or how much they have sinned, they are invited to call upon God. Women of worship, rejoice in the Lord!

The second lesson from the well is that your test may become your testimony. The fruit of God's revelation is a blessing to be shared. Be available and prepared to share with others the personal revelation of God, which enables the personal revelation of self. Many of us come to the well because someone shared his or her experiences with us. We believed their testimony. The testimony revealed the God of alternative endings. The God who heals, delviers, and breaks into human existence. It is a testimony that tells of a God of another chance who forgives the past and opens the door to a bright future.

The third Well Lesson is that you are a woman of value and a woman of worth. Jesus wants to share the message with you. Monique was convinced of her own worthlessness and tried to convince others of the same. She deserved everything negative that happened to her. Every harsh word spoken to her was earned. Every defeat was expected. She failed to rise to any challenge because she was convinced that she didn't deserve victory. She made herself the brunt of every bad joke. She held herself up to public ridicule. No one had a chance to think more of her because she was so busy trying to help him or her think less. Monique needed to come to the well quick!

Monique is worth the effort and so was the Samaritan woman. The Divine interrupted his journey for her. He submitted to an altered travel agenda. He stopped by an ancient well while he was teaching and touching on the way to a kairos appointed on a cross. He had already left his home in glory and soon He would die for sinners like her, Monique, you, and me. Jesus did all of this because we are worth it! We are often the last to know what the Lord has known all our lives. You are a woman of value and a woman of worth. Don't forget it!

The fifth Well Lesson is that everyone does not have a theophany like Moses, Elijah, Peter, John, or the Samaritan woman. But you can go to the well. How do you get to the well? The journey begins in prayer. It is expanded in worship and explored in study. It is empowered by fasting, demonstrated in service, and celebrated in praise. This is the yellow brick road that leads not to a powerless wizard in Oz, but to the King of Kings and the Lord of Lords!

Well Words

> *Worship the Lord in the splendor of his holiness, tremble before him, all the earth.*

PSALM 96:9

Come, let us bow down in worship, let us kneel before the Lord our Maker.

PSALM 95:6

. . . Worship the Lord your God, and serve him only.

MATTHEW 4:10B

And they stayed continually at the temple praising God.

LUKE 24:53

Worship the Lord with gladness; come before him with joyful songs.

PSALM 100:2

Enter his gates with thanksgiving and his courts with praise; give thanks to him and praise his name.

PSALM 100:4

"I will declare your name to my brothers; in the presence of the congregation I will sing your praise."

HEBREWS 2:12

Well Sabbatical

⌐ *Spend your sabbatical seasons in worship. First, set aside a daily time to spend in private worship. The presence of God is ushered in on the shoulders of praise, as God inhabits the praises of his people (Psalms). Praise is acclamation and adoration. It is verbally giving honor to God. If you are not quite sure how to begin, read praise passages from the Book of Psalms such as: "I will extol the Lord at all times; his praise will always be on my lips. My soul will boast in the Lord; let the afflicted hear and rejoice. Glorify the Lord with me; let us exalt his name together (Psalm 34:1–3). "Let me live that I may*

praise you . . ." (Psalm 119:175) or the praise crescendos of
Psalm 145–50.

⟶ After praising God, thank God for who He is, what He has
done, and what He is doing. Use Psalm 103 to begin your
time of thanksgiving. "Praise the Lord, O my soul; all my in-
most being, praise his holy name. Praise the Lord, O my soul,
and forget not all his benefits—who forgives all your sins and
heals all your diseases, who redeems your life from the pit and
crowns you with love and compassion, who satisfies your desires with good things so that your youth is renewed like the
eagle's" (Psalm 103:1–5).

⟶ Do not ask God to do anything for you. Save your prayer requests and concerns. Spend the balance of your sabbatical in
private worship reaching for the heart of God in praise and
thanksgiving, not petitioning.

Well Language

⟶ I am a woman of value.
⟶ I am a woman of worth.
⟶ I will praise the Lord at all times!
⟶ With my whole heart will I praise the Lord!
⟶ Magnify the Lord with me and together we give God praise!
⟶ Give God the praise!
⟶ Worship is my strength.
⟶ God is a spirit and I worship him in spirit and in truth!
⟶ Worship is my reach to God, blessing is the return.
⟶ God looks beyond my faults to my needs.
⟶ Lord, I am available to You!
⟶ I love the Lord!

⁓ *I can worship! Come magnify the Lord with me!*
⁓ *I will praise the Lord with my whole heart!*

Well Work

1. *Make the decision to attend a corporate worship setting of your choice. If you usually attend Sabbath worship, attend a midweek service during the day or evening. Spending time with Jesus in worship is an experience in revelation.*
2. *In your journal, write a love letter to the Lord. Share why you love the Lord, including a list of the many ways you can demonstrate your love for the Lord. Be open and honest, and express yourself fully.*
3. *Read I Peter 2 and list what the Bible says about you.*
4. *Look up Vessels of Honor in the concordance of your study Bible or Bible dictionary.*
5. *Create your own valentine for Jesus and add it to your collage.*

12
A Woman with a Purpose

*Then, leaving her water jar, the woman went back to the town
and said to the people, "Come, see a man who told me
everything I ever did. . . ."*

JOHN 4:28-29

My mother said I was a late bloomer. All the other flowers had blossomed. Their colors were brilliant, petals exquisite and fragrance intoxicating. Vashti was still budding.

All the other girls seemed so advanced. They wore bras and I was still in undershirts. They stayed up until ten and I was in bed by 8:30 P.M. They wore makeup and I wore Vaseline. They got perms and my hair was still pressed and curled on Saturday night in the kitchen. They wore Alberto VO5 and I was plastered with Dixie Peach. They wore stockings and I wore ankle or athletic socks. They applied to law school, took Med-Caps, joined the Peace Corps, ran for president of the student government association, or launched out into the deep while I sat at the starting gate writing poems for "The Preferred Spot." My mother said I was a late bloomer.

I preached my trial sermon at Bethel AME Church in Baltimore. My friends and family sat in the congregation thinking I had lost my mind. At any moment I would snap out of it.

I was very nervous and very scared. I arrived late and dressed wrong—a pale lavender calf-length dress instead of AME regulation black suit and white blouse. I hadn't slept well that week and I wasn't sure about my sermon which I had typed and retyped all morning. I stalled at the starting gate.

As I mounted the pulpit, my knees would not stop shaking. My hands went cold and my mouth got dry. I didn't doubt God—it was me I was worried about! I prayed and began to preach. The positive, jubilant response of the congregation startled me but I had learned in my piano lesson days that "Once begun, you don't stop until done!" When the sermon was over, I knew what I was born to do.

Conversion was my invitation to the well. The call to preach was my teachable moment, where I was able to face self and God. The trial sermon was a defining moment. I was a second-career preacher, a late bloomer, but nevertheless in full flower.

In the late morning of my life, I was no longer becoming but coming to terms with my Created Purpose. Now all of my experiences made sense. What seemed to be diverse, jangling parts of my assorted challenges and careers, education and experiences, travels and tribulations, business and blessings, marriage and motherhood, I now knew were all connected to my Created Purpose.

The Samaritan woman had a defining moment at the well when she faced herself and the Son of God. She realized that she was a woman of value and worth and that her past was not held against her. She now had something powerful to share. She immediately ran back to her village and convinced the community to return with her to the well to meet this man Jesus, who had told her everything she had ever done. This pass-around woman with a tainted lifestyle not only knew who the Messiah was but chatted with him at the well. The Divine was present in her situation. Things had not changed, she had. He was present in her circumstances, and we all want the Divine to be present in the time of trouble. If he doesn't change our lives, he will change us to handle our lives. This desert dweller had to be someone very special, for Christ would not spend precious moments on the unimportant people in important times. Jesus validated her, and her stock in the community rose considerably that day. She was compelled to share the good news; her revelation must have been dramatic because the same people who had gossiped and looked down on her before, now came to the well with her, in the heat of the day, to see and hear this Jesus for themselves. The woman at the well had found purpose in life beyond mere survival.

Defining moments are explained in this chapter as moments that have the power to change you: They can reveal the purpose that weaves through every aspect of who you are and what you do. Defining moments are life changing, and when they arrive your attitude toward them determines the outcome—are you open or aren't you? Defining moments can be like visions that speak of things to come. They can be like flashbacks, revelations gained through retrospect. They can also be breakthroughs like spiritual telegrams sent to affirm God's Created Purpose for your life. Remember God's Word: I know the plans I have for you, plans not to harm but to prosper you! Your defining moments reveal to you a vision and that vision becomes your destination. Vision reveals the destination of your Created Purpose. Where are you going in life? What is your vision for reaching your destination? Can you trace the threads of purpose in the fabric of your life that reveal your Created Purpose?

DEFINING MOMENTS

Jesus fell silent. The disciples said nothing, and the woman contemplated everything. The Samaritan woman was standing in the middle of a cataclysmic moment in time when what she knew fell away and was no longer valid. It was a defining moment for her precipitated by a conversation with Jesus at the well. She had journeyed through her anonymity. She had rejected surrendering her life to a surrogate. She broke through historical barriers of race and gender. Her fantasy shield fell, and she saw herself reflected in the eyes of Christ. Jesus sent her back to deal with her history so she could move on. The past was too heavy to carry to the future. Tomorrow has enough challenges without bringing the past along. She now had a personal revelation of the Son of God, a life-changing experience, a conversion. There was nothing more to say. It was a defining moment. The Samaritan woman dropped her water jar, willing to let go of what was no longer adequate. The water jar was suitable for water, but not for what she had to do now. It was useful for the person she had been, not for the person she was becoming. Running into the city, right back into her source of pain, she did not hesitate in returning to the place of rejection to turn it into a place of revival.

Part of personal transformation is not only resolution, but also reconciliation. The Samaritan woman had faced the Messiah, had faced her past, had faced herself, and now she was ready to face her community. The true test of personal transformation is the willingness to go beyond personal worship and beyond one-on-one personal experience with Christ. It is a willingness to share with others in the community what has been learned in private. She returned immediately to share the personal experience she had found at the well. She did not return to point fingers of blame or rehearse old hurts; rather she went back as God's testifier to a skeptical community. She went to the well because of what she was trying to avoid and she left the well because of what she was trying to achieve.

As I discussed in *Strength in the Struggle,* defining moments can arrive quietly or dramatically, when we are young or not-so-young. Dr. Benjamin Carson is Johns Hopkins Hospital's world-famous surgeon who led the surgical team that separated German Siamese twins joined at the head. His defining moment did not come in the operating room, but in the streets of Baltimore when he was a young boy and nearly killed another boy with a knife. The boy's belt buckle stopped the blade from penetrating his stomach. It was a defining moment that shook Dr. Carson to his very core. He turned from a negative street life to a positive lifestyle. He now uses a knife to save lives rather than take them.

Experience shapes you. On these ordinary trips to your well come the unexpected—and extraordinary—defining moments of your life. Defining moments are more than mere events or occasions; these moments have the power to change your life forever. Your life before defining moments and after defining moments is different. You think differently, feel differently, and act differently. Your view of life is different and perceptions are changed. Defining moments create the critical mass from which new habits are born. Priorities change because this dramatic pause in your life forces you to examine what is really important.

Jim and Jill Kelly had one hope. They wanted a son. When Hunter was born with a rare type of muscular dystrophy, the experience was a defining moment. It could have been a last things situation, except that the Kellys decided to ask the Divine to meet them where they were, at a kairos moment. The Kellys needed to develop a new way of thinking. This unexpected health issue motivated the Kellys to start a foundation they called Hunter's Hope to educate people about the rare disease. Their goal was to raise funds to help find a cure. Instead of making excuses they turned their misfortune into an opportunity to nurture, teach, and assist others connected to and affected by muscular dystrophy.

Alex Haley's defining moment came while listening to the stories of his ancestors, which were passed on from one generation to the next. He traced these ancestral stories and preserved them in his widely acclaimed book *Roots*. Mr. Haley was determined to learn about his heritage, and in the process he was able to face more of his past than many people ever will.

Osceola McCarty was denied a full education. She was pregnant with the possibilities of God, but her defining moment came when she dropped out of school in the sixth grade to take care of her ailing aunt. By the time her aunt died, it was too late for her to go back to school. All she could do was make a career washing and ironing other people's clothes. When her health forced her into retirement, she decided to divide her savings between herself, her family, her church, and the University of Southern Mississippi. The hardworking retired woman gave the college $250,000, even though she never visited nor attended the school. She may not have gotten the education she'd always wanted, but she was not ignorant; she was going to use her money to enable others to have the opportunity she never had. In the process, she'd be breaking down a few barriers too. She wanted other children to have what she had not had, a college education. She did it all by herself, without a husband or a car. Her vision became the destination of her Created Purpose.

Defining moments can be specific and personal, such as a divorce or the death of a spouse, parent, or child. Or they can be ordinary things that most people experience such as getting a first job, going on a date, being fired, taking a first airplane ride, or going to the well for water. Defining moments are ordinary experiences with extraordinary results. They can be catastrophic life-threatening situations—an earthquake, hurricane, tornado, or flood—or they can be other accidents that threaten the body, mind, and spirit. Defining moments can be communal or societal. They are formidable moments that impact not only the individual, but also groups of people within a society, affecting a segment of the community or the entire population for generations to come.

What are your societal defining moments? It could have been the Senate hearing on Justice Clarence Thomas's appointment to the Supreme Court. Professor Anita Hill's charges of sexual harassment ricocheted across the country, changing workplace etiquette for future generations. The Great Depression was a defining moment for millions who lost jobs, homes, and families to economic disaster. World War I, World War II, the Korean War, the Vietnam War were all defining moments for those men and women who fought and those who waited for their return. Apartheid and the Holocaust: These tragedies represent times when people were denied their personal freedom, their civil and human rights. The seeds of mistrust, fear, low self-esteem, anger, and exploitation were sown deep by the trauma of enslavement. The seed continues to bear with defining moments triggered by consistent racism and sexism.

The assassinations of John F. Kennedy, Robert Kennedy, Martin Luther King, Jr., and Medgar Evers were defining moments for the children of the Civil Rights era. The assassination of Tupac Shakur and Biggie Smalls are defining moments for members of Generation X. While baby boomers lit candles, cried, and held vigils for the Kennedys, King, and Evers, the hip-hop generation did the same for their fallen heroes. The sudden untimely deaths of Diana Princess of Wales, Selina, John F. Kennedy, Jr., his wife, Carolyn Bessette, and her sister, Lauren Bessette, are defining moments for many living in the last days of the twenty-first century. On September 11, 2001 the twin towers of American economic power crumbled and the symbol of American military might was penetrated by terrorist attacks. Thousands of innocent people perished at the World Trade Center and the Pentagon from commercial aircrafts used as deadly missiles. One plane crashed in a Pennsylvania field, missing its target but killing everyone on board. The world watched in horror, as this became the defining moment of the twenty-first century. The pages of this new millennium are now stained with the indelible blood of the innocent and the guilty. In a few short hours on a sunny morning in September, everything changed and nothing will ever be the same again.

Priorities changed as family and home once again took center stage. Churches, synagogues, mosques, and temples filled with those seeking relief, refuge, and retreat. Separation of church and state took a back seat to a National Day of Prayer. People hugged a little tighter and spoke more. People resolved not to leave home without saying at least "I love you!" because the day, we were reminded, could bring anything.

An old fear was resurrected in a new time. The same fear that motivates lynching, genocide, ethnic cleansing, prejudices, bigotry, racism, classism, and sexism in their worst forms rose from its pit. We watched it live, replayed and in living color, a million times. Many realized once again that growing old is not guaranteed. Time is to be treated like gold and days like precious diamonds. "Teach us to number our days aright, that we may gain a heart of wisdom" (Psalm 90:12).

Defining moments are the context from which new hopes, dreams, and fear rise. Our relationships are affected by defining moments. Our parenting, job performance, emotions, social consciousness, self-esteem, value, worth, psyches, and faith are all affected by defining moments. Conversion, the process that transforms belief and behavior, is a defining moment. It is a revelation. It is the well from which a river of Living Water springs. In this river flow Eternal life, the fruits of the Spirit, the compassion of Christ, faith, and the power to witness.

The well woman's transformation must have been so extraordinary that even the men in her community believed her right away. Her entrance was bold, her testimony powerful. They listened and followed her back to Jacob's well to listen themselves. She had found her voice, and the disciples found theirs. It was an experience of revelation, opportunity, and purpose all wrapped up in one moment. It was a kairos moment.

VISION IS THE DESTINATION OF PURPOSE

As the Samaritan woman left for the city, the disciples were concerned that Jesus had not eaten the food they brought him from town. They had left him hungry and tired and later found him engrossed in intimate conversation with a woman. Jesus speaks to them of a food that is not eaten from a plate. He says, "My food is to do the will of him who sent me and to finish his work" (John 4:34). He was receiving nourishment not from physical resources but from spiritual ones. The human drive to eat food is powerful, but Jesus indicated there is an even greater drive: the drive to do the will of God. To explain to the disciples what had happened, Jesus asked them to look at a nearby field of ripening fruit. The ordinary agricultural time between planting and harvesting had changed. The harvest was now ready. As they looked toward the fields, they may have seen the human harvest streaming from the city. The Hebrew agricultural calendar was divided into six cycles. It began with seed time and ended with harvest. In between were necessary intervals that were part of the growing cycle. The seed of salvation was planted in the Samaritan woman. The harvest or transformation occurred immediately, not after several intervals of the growing cycle. The woman planted the seeds of salvation by sharing the Good News in the city. Seed time and harvest met together for the first time. The Samaritan woman overcame learned ignorance and developed a new level of thinking in a very short amount of time. The seed planted in the woman was already producing. They had heard her sermon, the same one repeated again and again: "Come and see a man!"

I had a seminary professor who said we all have one sermon that we preach again and again. With every different biblical text and context, the sermon is the same: "Come and see a man." Come and see a man who is more than a role model and who helps us examine the concerns of our ambitions and achievements. Come and see a man who is more than a psychiatrist and who helps examine the concerns of our hearts and minds. Come see a man who is more than a priest and who serves as worship leader of rituals and intercession. Come and see a man who is more than a physician and who heals the body and the soul. Come see a man who is more than a prophet. Could this be the Christ?

The Divine encounter at the well gave the well woman courage to exercise her newfound significance. Many times we are able to feel significant, but have not discovered the Divine relationship that gives us the courage or confidence to exercise it. This woman found the power to choose her own direction, to go back to the city to give voice to the power to choose her own attitudes and values. She exercised the right to say no to reoccurring, self-defeating pursuits that would otherwise shoot her down faster than a repeating rifle. She uncovered an identity separate from all she had ever known before. Her Created Purpose grew out of her relationship with Jesus, not out of her habits, history, or heritage. She no longer lived by the expectation of others, but out of her Created Purpose. She was born to tell. Just as sure as a caterpillar is born to be a butterfly or the tadpole to become a frog, she was born to be a change agent. The raw material and potential are housed within our being. Habit, history, and heritage can deter or delay, distorting and even killing the seeds of significance locked within. Hazardous environments and predators can cause the mission to be aborted. But we all have a Created Purpose.

There are many women inside of you, but there is only one prime director. All of the other women are fed and nourished by her centrality. She is the main computer, the central headquarters, the hub of a wagon wheel, or the heart of a spider's web. This prime director connects all the others together like the threads of a spider's web. She touches all the other women like the spikes of a wagon wheel are all connected to the center. When she discovered her Created Purpose, the core of her existence, all the other women made sense. All the other women existed to be the diverse expression of the center or core. Jesus is the Son of the Living God; this is his Created Purpose. All other aspects of his being—Jesus the healer, the deliverer, the savior, the liberator, the justifier, the preacher, the teacher, the miracle worker, the forgiver, the reconciler—are energized by the core. One is not the sum total of all the others. All are representative of the core. When you identify your Created Purpose, all of the other women in your life will make sense. You will see how each woman is connected to the core and the role each woman plays in the process of your transformation and emancipation. You will see how each woman validates the others, how each woman feeds, nourishes or limits the others, and allows her own expression.

Created Purpose is the permanent thread that weaves through every aspect of existence. It is present in every thought, word, and deed. It is the answer to questions of "Why was I born?" and "Why am I here?" Purpose keeps you from meandering through life distracted by every event, person, or thing like Helene. It keeps energies focused on tasks and gives direction to vision. It helps you recover from disappointments and compels you toward completion. Created Purpose, coupled with persistence, breaks down barriers. The old story of the rock and the river explains the working of this dynamic duo. The purpose of the river is to run downstream. A large rock is in the way and the water pounds against the rock daily. Its continuous action cracks the rock. The river keeps pressing until the rock breaks, pushing until the rock becomes stones, the stones become pebbles, the pebbles become sand, the sand becomes silt, and finally, the rock becomes a part of the river itself. The river perseveres, not because it is strong, but because it is persistent. Purpose and persistence are a formidable pair.

In my short time living on Earth, I have done many things. I've been a sportscaster, color commentator, journalist, radio personality, radio station manager, television personality, public relations director, entrepreneur, and corporate vice president. When I faced God and myself at my own well experience, my Created Purpose became clear. I accepted God's call to preach his Gospel and pastor his people. All of the other women within me suddenly made sense. Each expression was an opportunity for learning and growth. As a model, I learned to be comfortable with crowds of staring people. As a journalist, I learned how to collect my thoughts and give them life. I learned how to survive the pressure of producing a daily story for a morning newspaper. I learned how to speak publicly while I was working on radio and television. I learned administration, leadership, and management from broadcast management. I learned balance, delayed gratification, and compromise as a wife and mother. I learned compassion at the foot of the cross. I learned how to endure when caught in the crossfire of racism and sexism. I learned that to live out my faith relationship with Jesus Christ was to preach and pastor from my own journey to the well. All my diverse experiences are summed up in my Created Purpose. Each woman is connected to the other. Each nourishes and supports my created core. Each is the sum of who I am, and who I am becoming.

The night of my trial sermon was not the only time God affirmed my Created Purpose. Just as God confirmed the covenant promise to

Abraham, then Isaac, Jacob, and the other patriarchs of the faith, the Creator continues to affirm our Created Purpose at significant times in our lives. The first Sunday I stood in the pulpit as the pastor of a congregation, arms raised in praise and thanksgiving, the Divine whispered in my heart of hearts: "This is why I was born." When I delivered a healthy baby girl who was being choked by her own umbilical cord, the Lord whispered again words of affirmation. When I held the hand of an elderly congregation member who was gasping for air on her deathbed and whispered in her ear that I loved her and God loved her best, I was again at the well. When I conducted the marriage reaffirmation service for a couple who nearly divorced, God spoke again. When I had to preach through and pray through hard times, the Lord reaffirmed my Created Purpose. When I stood in tears before a full Sunday sanctuary as God birthed the vision of the episcopacy in my heart, the Lord whispered ". . . for who knows that you are come to the kingdom for such a time as this" (Esther 4:14).

One of the first things a journalist learns is that every story must answer six basic questions: who, what, when, where, why, and how. You are the answer to the question *who*. The purpose is the *why*, and the vision is the *where*. Vision is the destination of purpose. It is an appointment with desired goals, or benchmarks of progress representing *what* you are doing with the purpose, your mission. It is *how* you are going to achieve your goals. A good place to begin uncovering your purpose is in prayer, fasting, and the Word of God. Our purpose is to serve God (Joshua 24:15). It is to seek God's kingdom first (Matthew 6:33); do the Father's will (John 4:34); finish the divine tasks (John 17:4); complete the mission joyfully (Acts 20:24); and become more like Christlike. We are to be like the salt of the earth, to season and preserve; the light to shine in the world so that others will see your good deed and praise your Father in heaven (Matthew 5:13–16).

Jesus did not leave his heavenly glories to come to Earth because he had nothing else to do. He came that we might have a more abundant life and to take away the sins of the whole world. What does it mean to live life on purpose? The purpose of the mechanic is different from the purpose of the driver. The driver's purpose is to turn the key in the ignition and drive safely to her destination. The mechanic is concerned with the response of the equipment used in the journey. The driver is concerned with getting to the end destination. The mechanic is concerned with the means to the end, making decisions that support the purpose of an end destination. So it is with us. Our purpose guides the goals, decisions, choices, priorities, and relationships of life, in relationship to our God-given purpose. The more time we spend with God, the more God can unfold our purpose. Jesus was in constant communication with his father. All that the father tells me, I do, he says in the book of Matthew. Jesus knew his purpose and lived his life to fulfill that purpose. His priorities were set according to his purpose and he did not forfeit his purpose for personal gain. When Peter wanted Jesus not to go to Jerusalem to suffer and die, Jesus said, "Get thee behind me Satan." He was not going to let Peter stand between him and the cross. His purpose was not to serve Peter's desires, but God's purpose for His life. When you don't know your purpose, then you serve others and their idea for your life, not God's intended purpose for you. On the eve of the cross, Jesus asked the Father one more time if there was any other way that His purpose might be achieved. His purpose kept him steady and on target, against all odds, until He had completed what He had come to do and could finally declare, "It is finished." There was a purpose to his coming, and when He had finished it, the Resurrection brought him home to the Father. Because Jesus lived on purpose, the way to salvation was completed. We too must be determined to live on purpose.

At times we are like professional pack rats, stowing away bits and pieces of our lives that are no longer useful: irrelevant people, places, and things. We hold on to crutches long after the break has been healed, to pictures of old boyfriends long after the breakup, to detrimental habits long after conversion, and to childish things long after maturity. The Samaritan woman released these symbols of survival to reach for significance. The pots represented the tools of survival; she found out that she had a greater purpose to fulfill. Compelled toward significance, her life was more than fetching and hauling water. She would become a significant catalyst for herself and others.

Like the Samaritan woman who is down to her last things with the hope that one day things will change, you too can be moved by your one hope as you carry on with your responsibilities in the midst of trials, get yourself to the well, and have a transformational experience with the Creator as you reconnect to the Divine in the ordinary moments of life. As you confront and overcome the problems and patterns of your past, remember: Resolved women are women who make decisions, not excuses. It may be the wrong hour, but if it's the right time don't let your kairos pass you by. Carry your weight by being your own birth mother rather than surrogating life away, and be resolved to live beyond dividing limitations. A different harvest requires a different seed. In the face of frustration, take some risks and accept the challenge to change as you reach for your higher self.

The goal of personal transformation is not resolution or reconciliation, but evolution. You evolve to your created center or purpose, a purpose poured into you while you lay in your mother's womb. It goes beyond DNA or a collision course between a sperm and an egg. It was spoken into you by God and fleshed out as you walked this Earth. God allows you to step into time for a season, until at the moment of kairos you return to your Eternal purpose like salmon swimming upstream to spawn. God will tell you when it is time, and the more you enter decisively into the path and discipline of your Created Purpose, the greater degree of reward you will reap. In other words, you reap what you sow. The more you put in, the more return you get on your investment. The caterpillar and the tadpole cannot ignore the call to change. The problem is that we can. The journey to the well is a call to change; it is a process.

The Samaritan woman's test became her testimony. The place of rejection became a revival for her and her community. She had already faced her past and survived to tell the victory. She had been in a mess and now could tell others that their messes did not have to be permanent. Sometimes your worst experiences become a testimony of triumph for others. Her life was changed and her experience would change others. She had a revelation and was now a woman of purpose. She had an opportunity, and she understood that her role went beyond hauling water, to being a change agent. The proclaimed, testator, and witness emerged to overshadow gender, habit, history, and heritage. It just didn't matter anymore. God would be there, wherever she went. The power of God-given purpose transformed her completely. She now had a future to look forward to, a future found in her encounter with the Divine at Jacob's well.

We all share the same hope: that one day things will change. Inside this Samaritan woman was a change agent pregnant with possibilities, a community catalyst that had the power to break down barriers and change her community, impacting its spiritual life for generations to come. As she listened, she discovered the power that comes when you are involved in a cause greater than you are. She was involved in something larger than herself. The woman overcame her past and went back to town with a vision of herself found in the eyes of Jesus, an appropriate evaluation of worth and value. She did not go back thinking more highly of herself, nor did she undervalue her existence; she now had a vision so potent that even if everything fell apart, her vision of who she was in Christ Jesus was stronger than anything others would think or say, and what society and her culture might conclude about her. It was bigger than rejection, and stronger than acceptance. It was time. No more excuses. She was going to seize the moment and follow her revelation. It doesn't matter what you are, but what you are willing to become. She was now willing to live life on purpose.

CALL TO ACTION

You are a woman of value and worth. Turn on the light: A revelation waits for you to make a difference in your world by clarifying your destination and living on purpose. You can become a change agent in your life, community, and world. Nurture opportunities instead of running away or hiding. You may just get in on a learning experience that changes your life. You can do it! Call upon God, the Creator, Redeemer, and Sanctifier, who will help you turn your test into a testimony. Come to the well of Living Water where vision is the destination of purpose and where you'll find belonging, acceptance, and love. Celebrate the woman of purpose you are becoming and always remember that you are a woman of value and worth!

Discipline of the Well

Well Lesson

The first lesson from the well is to pay attention to defining moments in your life—they can change you forever. By being aware, you can make the most of your intended purpose. A life before defining moments and after defining moments is different. The Samaritan woman discovered the power that comes when you are involved in a cause greater than you are. She became involved in something larger than personality and personal preference, and it was there that she discovered her purpose. She unwittingly played a significant role in God's plan of salvation. A woman unknown to many outside of Samaria becomes the lead character in a story told from one generation to the next. What a difference a defining moment made not only in her life but also in our lives.

The second lesson from the well is that your Created Purpose is the permanent thread that weaves through every aspect of your existence. If you know what your purpose is, just think how much more effective, fulfilling, and satisfying your life will be to everyone you come in contact with and to you personally. Purpose is present in every thought, word, and deed, and it is the answer to questions of "Why was I born?" and "Why am I here?" Purpose, coupled with persistence, breaks down barriers. Our belief initiates and guides our action. Knowing your destination significantly increases the chances of arriving where you want to end up.

The third lesson from the well is that as the cycles of life ebb and flow, as our circumstances change and new well moments present themselves, the journey continues. It is the will of God that seed time and harvest come together for personal communal salvation.

Well Words

And we know that in all things God works for the good of those who love him, who have been called according to his purpose.

ROMANS 8:28

. . . I have raised you up for this very purpose, that I might show my power and that my name might be proclaimed in all the earth.

EXODUS 9:16

Many are the plans in a man's heart, but it is the Lord's purpose that prevails.

PROVERBS 19:21

. . . so is my word that goes out from my mouth: It will not return to me empty, but will accomplish what I desire and achieve the purpose for which I sent it.

ISAIAH 55:11

Now it is God who has made us for this very purpose and has given us the Spirit as a deposit, guaranteeing what is to come.

2 CORINTHIANS 5:5

It is fine to be zealous, provided the purpose is good, and to be so always and not just when I am with you.

GALATIANS 4:18

In him we were also chosen, having been predestined according to the plan of him who works out everything in conformity with the purpose of his will.

EPHESIANS 1:11

. . . then make my joy complete by being like-minded, having the same love, being one in spirit and purpose.

PHILIPPIANS 2:2

. . . for it is God who works in you to will and to act according to his good purpose.

PHILIPPIANS 2:13

. . . who has saved us and called us to a holy life—not because of anything we have done but because of his own purpose and grace. This grace was given us in Christ Jesus before the beginning of time, . . .

2 TIMOTHY 1:9

Well Sabbatical

⁓ *Remember that the degree to which you pursue your rest period is the degree of the reward you receive for the time spent with the Lord. All too often we allow whims, fancies, and de-*

sires to lead us in doing, before we know the why of our doing. Use the scriptures from Well Words as you seek the Lord's guidance to Created Purpose identification. God is not playing a game, keeping purpose a mysterious secret.

Well Language

⌒ Think decisively; live on purpose.
⌒ My purpose is the why God created me.
⌒ Get involved in a cause greater than yourself.
⌒ It is not who you are but who you are willing to become.
⌒ I will take purpose and persistence wherever I go!
⌒ Competence needs courage and confidence to perform.
⌒ There is a reason to my being! I will live on purpose.
⌒ I will decide not to make excuses!

Well Work

1. Take the next few days to identify the permanent thread that is woven through every woman on the inside of you. Kevin W. McCarthy describes an excellent method of uncovering purpose in the book The On Purpose Person. In it he suggests making a want list in eight different categories. The topics include spiritual, financial/material, family, vocation/career, social/community, mental/intellectual, physical/health/recreational, and other.

2. Write your list of wants as fully as possible, consolidating categories if necessary. In each category compare the wants with one another to determine which is more important than another until you get down to one core want in each category. The author then suggests that you next compare the core want in each category until you identify one that is more important than the

other eight. The final core is your main purpose. The exercise is not final. It can be repeated.

3. Complete your collage. Focus on adding the items that reflect your created purpose. I added a cross, my favorite scipture, a butterfly (a great symbol for transformation), and the church bulletin from one of my first congregations.

   If you read this book with other women, you can have a collage party. Invite the others to bring their collage and a dish to share. (Yes, make it pot luck.) Each woman in turn shows her collage. She may give as much information as she desires. You may want to give small gifts for the collages that were the funniest or the most creative, unusual, spiritual, or unique.

   If you journeyed alone, have a collage party. Invite other women and share your collage and your journey. It may interest them to journey with you. In the end, you may frame your collage, keep it with your special treasures or never share it at all. It is your collage that respresents your personal journey to the well.

4. Your last assignment is to write your own poem or story of personal transformation. It is your declaration of freedom in Jesus Christ. It is your dialogue. It is your Magna Carta of self-definition and spiritual actualization.

   One of the participants in the Circle of Love wrote this poem at the end of her journey:

I took a Journey to the Well to discover me
Scared of what I may find
Anxious to discover the hidden things in me.
What did I find at the well?
The Lord waiting for me.
To help me to discover me.
At the well I found me.
A new me. A preacher in me

A scared child in me
A mature woman in me
A Journey to the well I took within me
A Journey to a well will always stay with me.
A Journey to a well to discover me
A Journey to a well shall always be with me.

Epilogue

*Many of the Samaritans from that town believed in him
because of the woman's testimony....*

JOHN 4:39

I would have liked to know the end of the Samaritan woman's story. The Scripture is silent about what happened after that hot afternoon at Jacob's well outside of the city. Did she resolve her living arrangements with a man to whom she was not married? Did she ever settle down to a committed relationship or give birth to children, as she gave birth to new possibilities and opportunities? Did she spend the remainder of her days telling people about this man, the Messiah she met at the well?

All we know is that an ordinary journey to fetch a pail of water was transformed into a defining moment of theological consequences. She traversed the trail of transformation and was personally blessed. The blessing she received from her theophany, a close encounter with the Divine, was not for her alone. It was greater than one woman, it was for her community and subsequent generations.

This woman was now living a decisive life. Once she made the decision to believe that this stranger who spoke to her intimately was the Messiah, she made a decision to act on her Created Purpose. To live a decisive life means you have made a decision to live on purpose as Kevin McCarthy writes in his book *The On-Purpose Person*. It means that all of your actions, behaviors, thoughts, and attitudes serve to support that decision. Those things that undermine the decisions are put aside and those things that undergird the decision are preserved.

It is like the football coach telling his receivers to make the decision to hold on to the ball. Everything they do in the game supports the decision to hold on to and not fumble the ball. The coach uses positive instruction that encourages faith not fear. It may sound easier to tell the receivers not to drop the ball. This is negative instruction whereby the positive statement encourages self-fulfilling prophecies. Positive well affirmations and the powerful Word of God encourage the heart, nurture the soul, and promote a can-do attitude.

Decisive living demands that you make decisions—they may be tough ones but make them. Indecision leaves decision in the hands of fickle fate or the whims of others, including culture, society, history, and heritage. Remember we want to make our decisions based on faith, not fear. I've decided to hold on to rather than drop the ball in my life. I decided because I believe, not because I am afraid. Fear is not all bad. Fear may keep you out of danger or trouble sometimes. It is the debilitating kind of fear that keeps you from ever going to the well or going to distant wells away from the rejecting eyes of the community.

The touch points of a decisive life are our final lessons from the well. The first lesson is that once the Samaritan woman allowed her purpose to lead her to a decision for Christ, she left what she was doing to do what she had been created to do. She became a trumpet sounding her one sermon, "Come and see a man who told me everything I ever did." Jesus changed her job description from water hauler to proclaimer. He just may do the same thing for you.

Do not despise the days of water hauling. They prepare you for the proclaiming. Everything prior to her well kairos moment prepared her for the moment of truth. She probably never dreamed that she would preach to her neighbors just like I never dreamed I'd superintend work in Africa as a bishop in the AME Church.

The second lesson is that God sent her back into hostile terri-tory. Jesus did not say "I'll fix everything for you!" She dropped her pots and went beyond her comfort zone to a people suspicious and reject-ing. The community had a track record with her and had caused enough pain for her to avoid regular contact. This time she was ready to handle the new confrontation. She left the city with gossip follow-ing her, and she returned with the Gospel and the people followed her to Jesus.

Jesus may send you back into your situation. He won't send you back until you are ready to handle the situation. It is just like Moses, who after forty years in exile in the Median desert was sent back to confront Pharaoh. When he returned, the enemies who could hurt him were dead and the others could not hurt him. God equipped Moses. He returned with a speech coach, Aaron, and a rod that he already had in his hand. The ordinary rod became an extraordinary tool in the hands of the prophet. It touched the ground and wood became a serpent. It touched the edge of the Nile and the water turned to blood. It touched the Red Sea and the water parted. Moses was sent back with a rod and a mission and Jesus sent the Samaritan woman back with a message.

The third lesson is that transformation demands a response. When the Samaritan woman changed, the people changed. Her trans-formation caused a different reaction from the people in her community. When your negativity is transformed into positive attitudes and actions, others cannot respond to you as they did before. As your self-esteem rises, others will perceive that it is no longer business as usual. As you drop harmful relationships, let go of painful memories, come to terms with the past, become your own birth mother to new possibilities, recog-nize your kairos and teachable moments and reconcile to Christ, your transformation will demand a different response. Some may be chal-lenged by the change; your change may frighten them. Regression will make them more comfortable. Progression fosters a different response. You have a choice: Fail and make them happy. Succeed and make God happy. Remember, when the Samaritan woman got right with God the people around her got right!

Daughters of the well, you have been drawn to the edge of the Living Water. Drink deeply and celebrate the woman you are becoming. The journey is not over, it is just beginning!

Vashti Murphy McKenzie

Recommended Reading

Essex, Barbara J. *Bad Girls of the Bible: Exploring Women of Question-able Virtue.* Cleveland, OH: United Church Press, 1999.

Hollies, Linda H. *Jesus and Those Bodacious Women: Life Lessons from One Sister to Another.* Cleveland, OH: United Church Press, 1998.

———. *Mother Goose Meets a Woman Called Wisdom: A Short Course in the Art of Self-determination.* Cleveland, OH: United Church Press, 2000.

———. *Taking Back My Yesterdays: Lessons in Forgiving and Moving Forward with Your Life.* Cleveland, OH: Pilgrim Press, 1997.

McCarthy, Kevin W. *The On-Purpose Person.* Colorado Springs, CO: Piñon Press, 1992.

McKenzie, Vashti M. *Strength in the Struggle: Leadership Development for Women.* Cleveland, OH: Pilgrim Press, 2001.

Produced in association with Urban Ministries Inc. (UMI), *Journey to the Well* is self-enriching for the individual reader as well as an empowering tool for group study. The UMI *Journey Reading Group Kit* includes a discussion leader's guide and student workbook. Contact UMI at 800-860-8642 to order your copy today.

FOR THE BEST IN PAPERBACKS, LOOK FOR THE 🐧

In every corner of the world, on every subject under the sun, Penguin represents quality and variety—the very best in publishing today.

For complete information about books available from Penguin—including Penguin Classics, Penguin Compass, and Puffins—and how to order them, write to us at the appropriate address below. Please note that for copyright reasons the selection of books varies from country to country.

In the United States: Please write to *Penguin Putnam Inc., P.O. Box 12289 Dept. B, Newark, New Jersey 07101-5289* or call 1-800-788-6262.

In the United Kingdom: Please write to *Dept. EP, Penguin Books Ltd, Bath Road, Harmondsworth, West Drayton, Middlesex UB7 0DA.*

In Canada: Please write to *Penguin Books Canada Ltd, 10 Alcorn Avenue, Suite 300, Toronto, Ontario M4V 3B2.*

In Australia: Please write to *Penguin Books Australia Ltd, P.O. Box 257, Ringwood, Victoria 3134.*

In New Zealand: Please write to *Penguin Books (NZ) Ltd, Private Bag 102902, North Shore Mail Centre, Auckland 10.*

In India: Please write to *Penguin Books India Pvt Ltd, 11 Panchsheel Shopping Centre, Panchsheel Park, New Delhi 110 017.*

In the Netherlands: Please write to *Penguin Books Netherlands bv, Postbus 3507, NL-1001 AH Amsterdam.*

In Germany: Please write to *Penguin Books Deutschland GmbH, Metzlerstrasse 26, 60594 Frankfurt am Main.*

In Spain: Please write to *Penguin Books S. A., Bravo Murillo 19, 1° B, 28015 Madrid.*

In Italy: Please write to *Penguin Italia s.r.l., Via Benedetto Croce 2, 20094 Corsico, Milano.*

In France: Please write to *Penguin France, Le Carré Wilson, 62 rue Benjamin Baillaud, 31500 Toulouse.*

In Japan: Please write to *Penguin Books Japan Ltd, Kaneko Building, 2-3-25 Koraku, Bunkyo-Ku, Tokyo 112.*

In South Africa: Please write to *Penguin Books South Africa (Pty) Ltd, Private Bag X14, Parkview, 2122 Johannesburg.*